RED IN THE CENTRE

Looking for the H Chord

MONTE DWYER

Monyer Pty Ltd

RED IN THE CENTRE
Looking for the H Chord

Published by
Monyer Pty Ltd

Ph: 0412 422 699
Email: info@monte.com.au

This edition published 2015
Copyright © Monte Dwyer 2011

The moral rights of the authors have been asserted.

ISBN: 978-0-646-55386-3

Printed in Australia by McPhersons Printing Group

10 9 8 7 6 5 4 3 2

To Jules & Rob

and dedicated parents everywhere
for the sacrifice of raising our children

ALSO BY MONTE

BOOKS:
Slapped by an Angel
Red in the Centre – *The Australian Bush Through Urban Eyes*
Red in the Centre – *Through a Crooked Lens*
Red in the Centre – *The Nomads at Large*
The Means

PLAYS:
I Would've Written
Tadpoles
Son

VIDEOS:
Monte Dwyer's Flying Cirrus – *How I Learned to
Stop Worrying and Love the Weather*
Red in the Centre – *Through a Crooked Lens*
Red in the Centre – *Looking for the H Chord*
Red in the Centre – *The Nomads at Large*

MUSIC:
Self Titled EP
Red in the Centre EP
Red in the Centre CD

All product available at **www.monte.com.au** while stocks last.

CONTENTS

INTRODUCTION

I first met Monte in the early 1990s on the set of the *Today Show*, back when he was the minister for all things irreverent and outrageous. I think it's fair to say he changed the way we viewed television weather in this country. He was genuinely entertaining and always up for a laugh, especially at his own expense, and the "travelling weatherman" blueprint he developed then remains the industry standard today.

Fast-forward twenty or so years and he's still travelling the country, though these days for his *Red in the Centre* project, which I gather involves him living the dream on the road (regardless of his claims of hardship and toil,) and writing stories about his adventures as he goes. However to categorise the stories in *Looking for the H Chord* would surely be misleading, for the moment you think you've got one bagged as a fine turn of subjective journalism, out pops a comical account of one of his misadventures, or a whimsical opinion piece about something he sees amiss out there. But the one thing they all are, is damned good reading. Like all the best Australian travel writers – Osmar White, Ernastine Hill, Frank Clune et al – Monte has a clear eye and a bright, enquiring mind, and when he tosses off a few casual lines on a matter you can almost hear the whisper of another thousand words left sleeping.

Yet he also has in his repertoire that most desirable of qualities in good writing – humour. For he is ultimately an *entertainer*, and he writes to delight. Barely a page goes by without some small joy for the attentive reader; a wryly observed absurdity, a totally original thought, an unexpected twist that sucks the laugh from your mouth like a plum. And he writes from the heart; he knows this country and its people like few of us do, and when they open up to him he repays their generosity by painting the warmest of portraits integrity will tolerate.

As a storyteller myself I find a lot to like about his stories. I like their freshness, their economy of style and their sense of fun. I like their contemporary timelessness and unashamedly Australian subject matter. Go Monte!

Peter FitzSimons
Neutral Bay, March 2011

THANKS

To *Australia Network* for providing a modest but steady stream of income while I sourced these stories – without that support Claude would surely have stopped the party long before this. To the people who graciously trusted me to tell their stories – I hope seeing yourself filtered through my cognitive burl isn't too much of a shock; I've tried at all times to repay your warmth in kind, but if I've taken liberties you don't appreciate I can only offer my sincere apologies – offense was never intended. To the people who buy my books, DVDs and CDs and allow me to remain creatively independent – a rare gift in these homogenised, profit-driven times. To the generous souls who hosted Claude and me at various times through the year, especially Paul and Christie Dickenson at Grungle Downs B&B in Darwin. To my patient photographer friend John Woodward for guiding my amateurish efforts with a camera, then polishing the fruits of my labours without criticism. And last but by no means least to my draft readers Terry Dwyer, James Mansfield, Iain Riggs and especially Ross Gallen, who all helped me see the difference between what I intended to write and what I actually wrote.

Cheers
Monte

PREFACE

People hit the road for all sorts of reasons.

Some do it while they're young and keen for adventure, perhaps encouraged by parents insisting they get out and make their mark while they still know everything. They travel in hired campervans painted with rude slogans or knockabout bombs bought in travellers' markets, and we call them backpackers and WWOOFers* and many things besides. They like to camp on the cheap in roadside stops, beachfront car parks and budget hostels, but they'll fork out for reef trips, wetland tours and every near-death experience they come across, and they're never far from a good party. One of their ilk said to me recently, "If you're not living on the edge, you're taking up too much space." I didn't mention there'd always be room created by blokes like him falling off; it's the duty of youth to be carefree. Blessed are the young for they remind us how to live irresponsibly.

Others do it for one last hurrah, perhaps encouraged by children insisting they get out and see the country while they can still see. They tend to travel in more comfort than the previous demographic, driving enormous campervans or towing muscly off-road caravans behind new 4WDs, and we know this group variously as grey nomads, the silver tsunami and SKIs**, again among other less flattering terms. This group also likes to camp in roadside stops and budget caravan parks, but they too spread their money near and far and they've taken the concept of "happy hour" to every forgotten

* Willing Workers On Organic Farms
**Spending the Kid's Inheritance

corner of the country. Blessed are the aged for they remind us how to die irresponsibly.

I live on the road because I eke a modest living out there. What category I fall into I couldn't say for certain, but I tend to call myself a professional vagrant or an itinerant bus driver depending on who I'm addressing, and I suspect "fool" will cover it whoever the audience. My work involves videotaping and editing short documentaries for *Australia Network* (and anyone else paying at the time), and writing and selling books and DVDs about my travels as I go. I drive a badly-behaved 4WD camperbus called Claude and camp as far from civilisation as possible. It's a thoroughly irresponsible and creatively rewarding lifestyle that I wouldn't swap for fame or fortune (unless they're on offer in small, manageable doses and then I reserve the right to change my mind). Blessed are the fools for they remind us that irresponsibility does pay after all, just not much.

The other reason I live on the road is because I'm looking for the H chord. For the uninitiated the H chord doesn't exist, except in some older forms of German and Northern European music where it's used as a substitute for the B chord. Some say the German baroque composer Johann Sebastian Bach coined the extra chord to avoid confusion over the number of Bs in a B flat notation, i.e. Bb. Others say he developed the H chord so he could weave his signature in progressive chords into his compositions, i.e. B,A,C,H. I say good on him either way: the great man sired twenty children and conceived such a magnificent body of work that we will be indebted to him for generations to come; we must cut him some slack.

But for me the H chord is a euphemism for the unobtainable.

It's not necessarily musical – though as a songwriter I am familiar with the agony of being an H chord short of a hit – rather it's that slippery something you just can't find when you need it most. I suspect I've been looking for it all my life. And here I go again.

AWAY

The last fun thing I did before I got away was run Claude into the back of some woman's car. It was just a glancing blow, really; smashed a taillight lens and scratched a panel. Hardly worth worrying about by my standards. Of course she didn't see it that way. Indeed her *criminal lawyer* partner – he made a point of introducing himself that way – rang me shortly afterwards to cross-check the details I'd given the woman, presumably to catch me out if I'd given false ID (because criminals are so dumb they always forget their cover immediately they leave the scene, and that's why all the bad guys are locked up and all the good guys are lawyers). It was a bit over the top and not far short of harrassment, but that's Sydney for you: everyone's paranoid about their goods and chattels. And to be fair I probably gave the woman cause for suspicion when I jumped out of the cabin loudly declaring my day was shaping up to be a beauty, all right, how about yours?

Then two days later I was being hounded by the woman's insurance company to provide my insurance details, resulting in a futile argument with the clerk about why I should give her that information before I saw a claim, since I wouldn't be using insurance if it was small. It sounded like qualification to me, i.e. if it was an insurance job the quote wouldn't be scrutinised. But the clerk was "having none of that nonsense" and the wheels on the bus went round, round, round…

This was getting weird. It was only a car accident, for Christ's sake; people have them every minute of every day all around the country. Sometimes Claude and I even manage two in one day!

Okay, so I admit I may not be one of Australia's best drivers, but I always clean up my own mess and I've never needed a lawyer's help, much less a *criminal lawyer*, or had a call from the other side's insurance company – on a *Saturday*, I might add – *before* the claim was lodged.

I realise some of you will sympathise with the aggrieved party here – there are two kinds of people in this world: car washers and environmental rationalists* – but for me it was yet another example of worshipping the empty fat pig. I don't know what cobwebby corner of my mind that came from but I'm sure you get my drift. This obsession we have with material things is not getting us anywhere good, and I don't even want to start on insurance companies.

It was high time I got out of the city.

Claude was as ready as he ever was, which is to say everything I broke on the last trip was now fixed, and everything else was ready to break in good turn. (You learn to be fatalistic driving a grey import.) I had the next book (*Through a Crooked Lens*) due from the publishers and the companion DVD to hand so I'd have new product for the next round. I had a fresh contract with *Australia Network* to supply another sixty *Postcards*. And in addition to the tangibles it was bearing down cold. While there are few cities in the world more agreeable than Sydney in the summertime, it doesn't do winter well. Sydney's an extrovert designed for outdoor living, and her people wilt indoors like daisies in the dark. Myself included.

Problem was I'd collected some baggage while I was busy trying to avoid it. As one of the last short, fat, bald sex symbols left on

---

*Those of us who reason it will rain eventually so there's no need to wash it.

the circuit I'd long considered it my duty to keep myself available, if only out of courtesy to my female fans. Furthermore the solitary nature of my work really didn't lend itself to having responsibilities of such a terrifying nature as a grown up relationship. But somehow I'd slipped into one without noticing, and now I was faced with the daunting prospect of trying to nurture the thing while I was on the road.

Don't get me wrong: she was lovely and funny and gentle and kind. But she was also completely nuts. I suspected she was even madder than me, though my friends thought that unlikely. And she laughed like a horse. Naturally I found her irresistible.

However it's one thing to be drawn to a fellow lunatic. It's an entirely different animal to maintain a long-distance relationship with one. Never mind the insanity, the logistics alone could bring it all undone. I was going bush with only sporadic mobile coverage to rely on, and my Big City Girl was rarely organised enough to have her phone: a) with her; b) charged up; c) in credit; and d) turned on (she turned it off whenever her creditors humbugged her with calls, which was regularly). The communication side of things didn't look promising.

But we thought it was worth a shot. After all, how much could possibly change in six weeks, when she was flying to Perth to join me for a week on the road?

I pondered this as I drove up the Pacific Highway.

WATER, WATER...

Southern Queensland was a treat. All through Balonne Country the land looked fat. Everywhere your disbelieving eyes ran lay great sheets of casual water and the rivers were running full. You couldn't see the cattle for the grass and you couldn't see the grass for the green; a stark contrast to the last time I came this way. I passed a couple of dingoes hung from a signpost and thought they were yellow pigs, they were so well-conditioned. And lining the road the rusty sorghum crops swayed heavily in the breeze, while plump cotton buds looked too white to be real. Unprecedented summer rains right through the centre had left this country in great shape.

I stayed a couple of nights at a caravan park in St George to do some IT housekeeping and generally get myself sorted for the trip, and the last thing I planned to do before heading west was top up my drinking water. I'd been using my own supply and figured I mightn't see fresh water for a while, so I pulled up beside the park's rainwater tanks and started unpacking my hose. Then along came the owner, built like a bulldog and angry like a hornet.

"You can't fill up here, mate," he said.

"Why not? The sign says 'drinking water'. What's it for otherwise?"

He shook his head and looked at Claude disdainfully. Obviously whatever it was for it wasn't for me. Whether he thought my tanks would be too big or I was a tosser for driving a bus with my face on the side I couldn't say, but he wouldn't let me have any water. I know Balonne River people can be very possessive about their water – see Cubbie Station* for a case in point – but this was beyond the pale. The tanks were full, the rain was still around and all I wanted was enough to replace what I'd used while I was a paying customer in his park. But the bulldog wasn't giving an inch. In the end I told him he could keep his water and left vowing to drown a voodoo doll in his likeness. Lucky for him I forgot.

Three hundred kilometres further west at the peaceful Cunnamulla Caravan Park the owner did let me fill my tank, so I decided to camp the night and "go downtown a while and see just what downtown could do for me".**

I met the young couple who'd just bought the local paper and watched them print and fold the week's edition, before joining them for a meal. He was a local boy who'd left to travel, before returning to look after the farm. He'd done his time as a journalist on the metropolitan papers and the discipline showed in his articles. The stories were crisp and clear and reflected a broader view than you find in most country newspapers. I asked him why he came back. "Just seemed the right thing to do," he said. "Made more sense than setting up somewhere on the coast."

He'd met his Australian partner in Paris and she had no background in journalism, but now she was as much a part of the paper as he. "It's supposed to be a Thursday paper, but we often don't get it out till Saturday," she laughed. "The locals lay bets on it."

I left him preparing the form guide for the upcoming yearly race

* Cotton property on the Culgoa River in Queensland famous for its innovative approach to water appropriation. Co-incidentally, as this book was going to print, the architect of the irrigation system, John Grabbe, was sacked under mysterious circumstances by the administrators of the property.

**Townes Van Zant – Blue Wind Blew

meet; a job, he said, that was more trouble than it was worth, but one they were happy to do to make their small contribution. "We inherited this job from the previous owner," he shrugged. "And someone's got to do it."

Further down the street I asked a few people about road conditions to the west, but the stories varied. Some told me I wouldn't even get to Innamincka, let alone down the Strzelecki Track; others gave me the very Australian "no worries mate; do it on a bicycle" kind of optimism. I decided I was too far away yet to get an accurate opinion.

Before I left Cunnamulla I drove out to the weir to see the rare sight of a million fingerlings trying to swim the falls. This only happens when the rivers are in heavy flood, and some weirs are kinder to the fish than others. Cunnamulla's is a death trap, with the drop too high for the fish to jump, the flow too strong to swim around and no fish steps built into the wall. So the fish are left to congregate in great numbers at the base of the falls to await death by fatigue, asphyxiation or bird: the herons, kites and spoonbills have a field day. Not surprisingly, scientists maintain that dams and weirs pose a significant threat to Australia's inland fish populations.

A little further west at Eulo I met a local who told me they have no such impediment on the Paroo.

"It's a pristine river system. No development, no obstacles for the adults going upstream to spawn, or for the fingerlings trying to migrate back up to colonise.

"Their natural instinct is to go upriver," he continued, "and when conditions are right – plenty of water, the right temperature – they spawn and the eggs float downstream to hatch and grow. And then in twelve months time we'll have some nice little pound, pound-

and-a-quarter Yellowbelly.

"The Paroo is the last river in South West Queensland that joins with the Darling – providing they're both in flood, like now – so anything that's in the Darling you'll catch in this one: cod, carp, Forky Tails, tortoises."

He's a jovial man who's lived on the rivers most of his life. He's wearing shorts, shirt and thongs, with a battered straw boater on his head. We're sitting on a dead branch on the banks of the river and behind us the water flows brown and steady, wending its way through the eucalyptus scrub. This country is renowned for its Yapunya tree honey and the flooding will mean a good season for the beekeepers, along with everyone else. I drew his attention to a flock of ibises working the shallows.

"Yeah, everything lives off each other," he nodded, smiling. "In good seasons, everything flourishes."

And the seasons don't get a lot better. The flood level peaked at 6.275 metres, breaking the previous highest record of 5.8 metres set at Eulo in both 1990 and 1974. Twenty years is a long time to wait between drenchings, but when it finally rains out here it doesn't muck about. And then, if the contentment on my local's face was anything to go by, all is forgiven.

As I continued west the story was the same: plenty of fodder, every hollow in the landscape a Johnny-come-lately lake and the rivers running strong. It really was a delight to see the country looking so rich. I asked the publican at Noccundra if it was as good as he'd ever seen it.

"It's as good as most people have seen it," he assured me. "Most times this is pretty bony, stoney country. But last week I went for a drive up the road and thought I was in Scotland!"

That's the natural cycle out here. See the land after rain and you imagine it could carry enough cattle to feed the world. The graziers build their stocks up and everyone's "in clover" as the old chestnut goes. Then as drought sneaks in like a thief the grass disappears and the farmers start de-stocking, and keep de-stocking down to the largest breeding herd they can sustain by hand feeding or feedlot. Then the rain comes – it always comes, eventually – and when the grass comes back the juggle begins to re-stock the land as quickly as funds allow. But then, of course, there never seems to be enough cattle around to take advantage.

"There's not enough cattle in the *country* to eat all the grass now!" the publican insists. "No, we can't help nature but it's a great problem to have."

Indeed. Unless you're trying to drive through it.

NOT THE CUNAMULLA FELLA

While I'm farting about in Cunnamulla looking for a story I find myself standing in front of the statue of the Cunnamulla Fella, the wallaby stew eating, brawling, bonking wag from the song of the same name by Slim Dusty and Stan Costa. Thinking it might be fun to go looking for the real deal, when I return to the Caravan Park I ask my host for her take on the story.

"A lot of people around town think the statue's not right," she says.

"How so?"

"His swag's too big and his package is too small," she answers with a grin almost as wild as her bright red hair. It's clear she's not talking about his tucker bag.

I decide it would probably work as a colour piece and fetch the camera. But as I'm leaving I stop to get a vox pop from one of my fellow residents in the caravan park and get completely waylaid in the process.

He's a large-boned man of about sixty-five, bald except for a band of greying hair clinging to the back of his head, and he lives in an old school bus stuffed so full of "rubbish" as he calls it, that he can barely get into the thing. When I approach with the camera he's sitting in all his bare-bellied glory in the sun, reading, and at the question of who the real Cunnamulla Fella might be he chuckles and offers to show me a trick. That's when he makes the first of his many forays to the top step of his bus to reach in and extract something from the clutter. He returns with a small, notched stick with a wooden propellor attached to one end.

"Ever seen one of these?"

"Can't recall it."

"It's a Huey Stick. Watch."

He runs the back of a spoon up and down along the notches till the vibration makes the propellor spin, then whistles and the propellor changes direction without him changing his spooning action. It's the sort of trick that would intrigue a ten-year-old greatly, but I'm more interested in the man. So just to play along I take the toy and show my ineptitude before returning it.

"Ten bucks and I'll give you one and show you how it's done," he says.

I admit I've paid more for less in my time but on this occasion my highest offer is a swap for one of my books. He accepts and then forgets to give me the Huey stick anyway, which I figure I can live without.

It's clear from the start that he's on his own cloud, this bloke; an outsider, a loner, to be treated with suspicion, I dare say, by the good citizens of town. He's old enough to have a history and there's bound to be some dirt in there somewhere, real or imagined. But who am I to judge? I'm sure I come under that category often enough. Indeed I'm sure we all do.

He tells me he's been wandering around the gemfields for a decade or more in his bus, mostly looking for opals. He's bailed up in Cunnamulla waiting to catch a bus to Brisbane for an operation on his foot. He tows a box trailer filled to overflowing with the overflow from the bus, and he has a forty-four gallon drum full of opal rough strapped to the frame. He travels alone and likes it that way.

"When did you first see this coming?" I ask him. "This lifestyle."

"When I couldn't settle down to married life, or the suburban life. This is what I wanted to do. I wanted some time out for *me*," he stresses, leaning forward and spanning his hand across his chest, hinting at plenty left unsaid.

"Married? Kids"

"Oh yeah, got all those. Lots of wives, lots of kids."

"The whole catastrophe."

"Yeah."

"How many kids?"

"Half a dozen."

"Ex wives?"

"Yeah, heaps a them."

I laugh and he sits back and crosses his arms, looking at me noncommittally.

"And none of them are interested in this nomadic life?"

"Didn't ask 'em. Didn't want 'em. Just like it on me own." He's still holding my gaze when he asks me if I've been married.

"Oh, I've had a couple of goes at it, yeah."

"Have ya?" he smiles a whiff.

"You've gotta have something to do when you're young and silly, haven't you?"

"It's not worth taking serious, but."

"No, you don't wanna take it up full time."

He's turned the tables on me and I notice we're sounding like a couple of old misogynists, and I'm not sure how much of my contribution is heartfelt and how much is to put my talent at ease. I've been told I'm something of a chameleon when it comes to communicating; one of my wives told me, as a matter of fact.

Apparently I tailor my conversation to the surroundings. If it's rough trade I use the vernacular and swear, with suits I smarten up and articulate, with women I tend to soften (or flirt if I'm in the mood). There's (usually) no intent there beyond getting on with people and I'm sure we all do it to some degree, but I've fallen in step with my talent here a little too readily for my liking.

"A lot of people seem to think it's very serious," he continues. "Wasn't very serious for me."

"Was it serious for your wives?"

"I don't think it was serious for any of them. They didn't seem to suffer much, you know? On and on they went."

"Well, I think we're all fairly resilient."

"We receive shocks about it but they don't."

"Women? You think they're more pragmatic?"

"Oh yeah. Choof off to the next one." He's still very matter-of-facto with his responses, as if he's thought them through long ago and doesn't really care what anyone else thinks.

"My old man told me once if it wasn't for kids you wouldn't bother," I say, noticing myself falling into step beside him again, and thinking it was probably just a throwaway line of the old man's anyway, because *he* certainly kept bothering. There are two dialogues going on here and I'm not sure I'm across either.

"Not my kids," says my misogynist friend.

"Why? Did they give you some grief?"

"Oh yeah. Lot's of grief. One fella joined the army. He was ten months in the Army and nine months in the stockade. So if the army can't do anything with them I don't want to try.

"My last wife always wanted to have children," he carries on. "Then she met mine and said she'd rather breed horses."

I laugh.

"It's true," he assures me.

"I don't doubt it. When did you leave your last wife?"

"Must have been about fifteen years ago. Just off-handedly; I don't know, really."

"And you haven't had any contact since?"

"Oh, no mate," he scoffs, as if I'd asked him if he'd like gonorrhoea. "Once having had a full dose of that sort of thing, you wouldn't go back for little doses, would you? Eh?"

He's a hard case. These aren't commonly expressed points of view I'm hearing here, even if some people do share them at times. He tells me he used to be a blacksmith at the shipyards, and fetches some opal he's polished up. There are some quality pieces, mainly in blues and greens, plus a lump of opalised wood and a few Yowah Nuts* as well. Then he retreats to the bus again and returns with more gems, this time in the form of a small bundle of photos.

"See, there's one you can't print," he says, offering me a shot of him modelling for an art class. He's sitting on a stool with his arms crossed on his chest, wearing a little white cap. Otherwise he's stark bollocky naked.

"That's a bloody beautiful shot mate," I say, trying to take it from his hand to put it on camera. He resists, but I can tell he doesn't really mind. "Come on, mate, you've gotta share that one."

"Go on, do what you will," he says, letting it go and waving me away.

Then there's a couple of him in drag – "It was a hen's party and that woman paid me to embarrass the bride" – and another

---

*Opal matrix inside an ironstone rock, commonly found at Yowah, Southern Queensland.

shot of someone's hand with grossly blackened fingers and nails – "That's all about drugs mate; injecting under the fingernails. She asked me to help her because I'm a Justice of the Peace. Said the hospital wouldn't help. But they're all liars, mate." – and several other intriguing shots he shuffles to the back of the pack before I can get at them. Like I said, he had a history.

Then somewhere along the way we get philosophical and start talking about the mortgage trap – "for Christ's sake don't get caught in that; tell them to keep their houses and live under a sheet of iron" – and the problems of living in the city – "everyone after money, trying to kill you…" – and absent friends – "all me old mates are dying now," he says with a sigh.

"I think it awaits us all, doesn't it? There's no escape is there?"

"I don't think so. I'll let you know if there is."

"So what do you think the trick is? Just enjoy it as much as you can?"

"You call it a trick? There's a poem about that."

"How's it go?"

> "'I must go down to the seas again, to the lonely
> sea and the sky,
> And all I ask is a tall ship and a star to steer her by,
> And the wheel's kick and the wind's song and the
> white sail's shaking,
> And a grey mist on the sea's face, and a grey dawn
> breaking.'"

He stops his recital and looks up at me. "You know that one?"

"I've heard it. But go on."

"The second verse is:

> *'I must go down to the seas again, for the call of*
> *the running tide*
> *Is a wild call and a clear call that may not be*
> *denied;*
> *And all I ask is a windy day with the white clouds*
> *flying,*
> *And the flung spray and the blown spume, and the*
> *seagulls crying.'*

And the last verse:

> *'I must go down to the seas again, to the vagrant*
> *gypsy life*
> *To the gull's way and the whale's way, where the*
> *wind's like a whetted knife;*
> *And all I ask is a merry yarn from a laughing*
> *fellow rover,*
> *And a quiet sleep and a sweet dream when the*
> *long trick's over.'"*

"Who was that?"

"Masefield*. English poet laureate. But I think my trick is nearly over."

"Do you think?"

---

*Sea Fever, from Salt-Water Poems and Ballads by John Masefield. Note: More learned scholars than this humble scribe have agreed that Masefield's 'trick' was a reference to a shift or term of duty on deck; but the analogy still works for me.

"Yeah, yeah."

"How much more time have you got?"

"Oh, few years I suppose."

"What would you like to do with that time?"

"Go to Western Australia and find lots of gold."

"What is it about the gems, the precious metals?"

"They're nice. I like 'em."

"Is it the promise of riches? At this stage of life that wouldn't matter would it?"

"No, just something to do…"

Till the long trick is over.

STUCK

Since the roads are closed from Noccundra to the Strzelecki Track and I'm ultimately heading for the Great Victoria Desert, I head south in the hope I may get an eleventh hour reprieve at Tibooburra. If there's no way west from there I'm faced with a significant detour south to Broken Hill then across and up, which is still better than making a big loop north through Boulia and across and down the Stuart Highway. When the rains cut roads out here, the long way around can be thousands of kilometres.

At the Bransby-Santos road junction I flag down a truck coming from the west and quiz him about the roads. The driver confirms what I've already heard: the Strzelecki Creek has cut all access and there's none looking likely in the near future. You can weave your way along the back roads to Innamincka, but that's the end of the line. And the Merty Merty road – my last resort – has also succumbed to the normally benign Strzelecki Creek. I carry on, hopes fading.

About fifty kilometres north of the NSW border I make camp on one of those unconnected waterways that only join up in exceptional years. It's longer than a billabong and shorter than a creek, and whatever you care to name the thing it's certainly a picture in the afternoon light. Mature Eucalypts line the banks casting rich emerald and gold reflections over the glossy surface, their gnarly old roots and dead branches twisting and stretching towards the water like slender brown kids caught in the act of diving into a waterhole. Here and there a partly submerged snag runs deep into the clear water, somehow giving the impression of permanence.

Though it's late in the season a pair of Mudlarks feed fledglings in the nest, and all around the birdlife is noisy and active as it makes final preparations for the night's roost. The lush ground cover is thick with grasshoppers and every footfall flushes a new squadron into the air, settling again after a short flight to return to the task of stripping the vegetation bare. As the light wanes the birds quiet and the crickets and frogs take up the tune, hesitantly at first, as one, then a second and another catches on, before the whole twilight chorus is playing at full volume, noisier even than the birds.

I light a fire and to pass the time while it makes coals I punch some holes in the bottom of my billy can and bait it with a chunk of sausage to see whether there are any cherubin in the stream. Instead I catch a couple of crabs! Where the hell they come from I've no idea. I've heard back hoe operators in these parts talk of digging out pockets of water deep in the soil, from which yabbies and shrimp and even fish have emerged; I can only imagine that's how the crabs survive the dry spells as well. I decide against trying to catch a fish on the grounds of laziness and return the crabs unharmed to continue their mysterious life cycles. By the time I've finished cooking and eating my dinner the darkness has muffled the sounds of another day passing and the night is settling in for its shift with a shuffle, a faraway screech and a gentle stirring of the wind.

The next morning I carry on down the Silver City Highway, a grandiose name for the two tyre tracks it is in parts, taking the well-established detours wherever the water still covers the road. At one less sinister-looking crossing I decide to give Claude a run in the mud. It's only about thirty metres across and the water isn't deep, and although there's a layer of ooze on top it has a hard base and looks do-able. Indeed there are fresh tracks where a vehicle has already gone through earlier, and I figure it's almost a better result for me if I do get stuck because at least then I'll get a story out of it. So I set up the cameras to cover that possibility and then take a shot at crossing. I miss, spectacularly. Even before I reach the water Claude slips off the road and buries his nose in the mud. I'm well stuck.

No problem; I'll just drive out. Claude is a 4WD, surely this is what he was made for. But for some reason I can't get any drive to the wheels. The motor is performing normally, but as soon as I engage the automatic transmission the revs drop to about five hundred and we just sit there. I've got no power under load at all; couldn't get pram wheels to spin. There's something seriously amiss, here, and I've no idea what it is.*

I get out and do a reccy. Claude's front passenger-side wheel is up to the hub in sludge, and the rear is in almost as deep. He's leaning perilously to the left and for a brief moment I enjoy the absurd prospect of him falling right over in the mud, but sober up quickly enough when I realise it wouldn't be the least bit amusing if it actually happened.

About a kilometre distant I can see the occasional vehicle using the detour road I should've taken, but decide against walking over and flagging down a tow in favour of videotaping the manual extraction. And that's exactly what it turns out to be: a manual extraction**. The mud is soft and heavy and about a third of Claude's underbelly is hung up in the bog. It's going to be a long

---

* I put this problem to every mechanic I encountered all around the country, but it took six months and over ten thousand kilometres to get it fully diagnosed. See page 227.

**Nursing term for the least savoury procedure used to cure constipation.

day on the shovel. But it's better to be self-sufficient in the bush than constantly expecting help, I tell myself, especially if you've been purposefully cavalier in the first place. I'm fairly sure that's bullshit at this point in time, but I still tell myself all the same.

Operating a camera and using a shovel are opposing skills. One demands you knuckle down and get grubby, the other requires attention to detail and cleanliness. It's an inelegant shoot to say the least. But the sun's shining and it's not unpleasant being out here under a vivid blue sky, making money out of a mistake. For the first hour. By the second hour I'm less convinced. I've exhausted all the usual tricks like shoving sticks under the wheels and letting air out of the tyres, and I've also calculated that I'm now officially working for a lower hourly rate than a council worker for doing the same job. I lean on my shovel for a bit to upskill.

Luckily after about two hours of juggling camera angles and muddy shovels a good-natured station hand from nearby Naryilco pulls up and offers me a tow out with the snatch strap. I accept graciously; quickly, I might add, but with great humility. It's one thing to be self-sufficient, but there's no point being rude about it.

Claude comes out of the bog like the other kind of medical extraction and we're back in business. I thank the Naryilco station hand and hit the road again, this time via the detour. An hour later I'm pulling up at the Family Hotel in Tibooburra and everyone already knows exactly how I spent the morning, proving the bush telegraph has even better conductivity in the wet. After a couple of lame attempts I give up trying to explain how I half-intended the bogging in the first place. Better they think I'm a fool for getting bogged than what they'd think if they knew I did it willingly.

CORNERED

Tibooburra is the north-westernmost town in New South Wales. It's hot, mostly marginal sheep country, with a bit of tourism thrown in to keep the town's 150 or so residents off the streets. A few years ago the Sydney Morning Herald newspaper ran a story about Tibooburra being the fastest growing town in the state. Apparently twenty babies were born in the one year. Locals blamed the drought. "There's nothing else to do," one was quoted in the article. The local MP was also quoted as being delighted Tibooburrans were "getting on with the job." Indeed.

Coming into town I wondered if the breaking of the drought would offer any new angles. Everybody loves a good *wink, wink, nudge, nudge* story, but innuendo alone won't carry it far. I needed strong talent and colourful speculation, and maybe even a few facts for the purists. So I asked around for a day or so but couldn't find a decent thread. Met some friendly people and learned a bit about the town's wild and woolly past, but heard little to substantiate the theory that Tibooburrans' breeding cycle was linked to seasonal conditions, like everything else's out here seemed to be.

What I did hear about, though, was an alternate route to the Strzelecki Track. It cut through private property on the western side of Cameron Corner and wasn't widely known, but it would get me around the worst of the flooding and into South Australia without taking a lengthy detour. Tibooburra had delivered after all. I left feeling well-disposed towards the town.

Which was just as well because I was back within a couple of hours. No sooner had my goodwill morphed into that weird kind of love men develop for their motor vehicles, when Claude broke down on me. Threw a turbo hose about eighty kilometres out and forced me to limp back to Tibooburra on half-ratpower. (Of course that diagnosis rolls off the tongue now, in hindsight, but at the time I had no clue what it was. Sounded like emphysema to me. So back I went for a second opinion.)

Luckily a couple of the boys from the National Parks depot identified the problem and re-connected the hose, and I was underway again without too much delay. I suspect they thought I was a dolt for a) being so obviously inept; and b) for going straight back out there in spite of being so obviously inept. But what else could I do? It is my work, after all. And anyway, I knew it was highly unlikely Claude would let me down again.

Naturally the bastard let me down again immediately, this time with a return of the old alternator problems. And this time the diagnosis came courtesy of the ranger and his son at Fort Grey National Park. They may be struggling to contain the feral infestations in our National Parks but they're surely churning out some handy bush mechanics. (Although it must be said this time I wasn't entirely clueless about the problem, that being the fifth alternator Claude had blown on my watch. Later that week, while I was waiting for a replacement to be flown in to Copley, a bloke asked if I'd been on the road long this time and I replied, "No, I'm only one alternator in.")

Anyway, I won't dwell on Claude's antics or I'll start weeping uncontrollably again. Suffice to say it was a full day's drive in either direction to any reliable service centre so I crossed my fingers, set my jaw and pushed on.

I was the sole visitor to Cameron Corner thanks to the perceived (rather than actual) road conditions. Normally by the Easter weekend the traffic through the Corner is in full swing, but news of roads being cut tends to keep most people away for much longer than the roads are closed. Unfortunately for the people whose livelihood depends on the travelling public, the media doesn't consider it a story when a road re-opens.

Cameron was the surveyor who spent two years of his life pegging the border between New South Wales and Queensland back in the late 1800s – imagine that: belting a peg in the ground every mile between the coast and a pre-determined point 1,300 kilometres into the desert, with no cold beer at the end, either – and these days an embellished white marker offers a photo opportunity at the junction of the three states (South Australia being the third), although the actual survey peg is about five metres away and easily missed.

The roadhouse, though, can't be missed, and is often described as the only Queensland business with a New South Wales postcode and South Australian telephone number. It was started about twenty years ago by a Vietnam vet called Sandy*, who sat at the Corner and counted cars for a day and decided there was enough traffic to support a business. A striking photo of him taken while in active service sits above the bar: young, bare-chested and bullet-draped if not proof. One can only imagine after an experience like Vietnam it would have made perfect sense to start a new life in a location like Cameron Corner.

"He just built a shed and started trading out of that," I'm told by Phyllis, one of the five current residents of the Corner. "Fuel,

*The video story aired in Asia flushed out one of Sandy's mates who served with him in Vietnam. He emailed me his thanks from Vietnam, where he was teaching school kids about kangaroos and other Australian icons. Another Vietnam vet changed forever.

beer – of course beer; that's Australian isn't it, you don't go anywhere without a beer… and just built it up from that. It's the only stop for about five hundred kilometres between Tibooburra and Innamincka."

These day's Sandy's no longer with us, but the steady stream of 4WD traffic through the season supports his decision, and it's a favourite pit stop with rallies and bashes. There's still fuel and cold beer along with meals and accommodation, and for the diehards and nut cases a rough, three hole golf course in the Queensland sector. There are plans afoot to develop a nine hole tri-state course – "just because we can," says Phyllis – but at this stage approval is still pending for use of the New South Wales section, which is on National Park land, except for a narrow strip along the dog fence under the control of the Wild Dog Board.

The dog fence is one of those fantastic creations you'd only find in Australia. It's a vermin-proof barrier designed to keep dingoes out of the sheep grazing areas of the south-east, and at well over 5,000 kilometres is by far the longest man-made structure in the world. While much of it wends its way in an irregular fashion through Queensland and South Australia, it hugs the north-west border of New South Wales for several hundred kilometres, neatly separating that state from the other two and visually enhancing the "cornered" look of Cameron Corner.

"One of the previous owners also started a New Year's Eve party here," Phyllis elaborates on the benefits of the location. "So now every year we start with a barbecue at the roadhouse, then we go to the corner peg and celebrate three separate New Year's Eves, at different times. So by the time you get past the third one you're pretty well tanked."

She's a jolly soul who likes the peace and solitude of remote locations, and we're watching her pet goats she's let out to graze on the new growth as we speak. There's a wether and two nannies all about half-grown, and they look highly vulnerable out here in desert country, prompting me to mention how lucky she is having a well-maintained dog fence to keep the dingoes out.

"Well, we're actually on the outside of the fence at the minute," she replies, graciously sliding over my gaffe, "so we're in dingo territory here."

I knew that, of course, just forgot to think before I spoke. In any case the effectiveness of the dog fence has often been questioned. Wild dogs are still a big problem within the protected zones, and many see trapping and baiting as more cost-effective alternatives. Yet others believe that without the fence there would be no sheep industry in this country. Either way it's still maintained, and later that day the two dog fencers whose separate boundaries meet at the Corner drop in for a coffee and a chat. Their names are Larry and Lloyd and they're a good double act. Larry's a fourth generation dog fencer and Lloyd's an ex-dairy farmer from Victoria who took the contract four years ago as a bit of a "sand change", but isn't looking to renew when it expires in a couple of weeks. I suggest the job would probably attract people running away from something, and ask what he was fleeing. "Cows," he replies without missing a beat.

They tell me they each get a hundred kilometres of fence to look after, and different states apply different regulations to their work practices. If Larry is working the National Park side of his run, for instance, he can't fill a hole under the fence with sand taken from the Park. Instead he has to cut the fence and fetch sand from the South Australian side. The insanity of bureaucracy manifesting even out here in the desert makes me wonder how they'll go replacing divots if they ever get the golf course happening.

But in the end it's always about the people and it's the two fencers I'll remember best about Cameron Corner. We're chatting over cups of coffee at the roadhouse and most of the time is spent laughing. Lloyd looks like an old surfie with white hair and a red face, and he's droll enough to make you listen closely to what he's saying. Larry has orange hair and a handlebar moustache, and by his own admission has had no real education and only knows the dog fence, but he's an agreeable soul and makes a good foil for Lloyd's wit.

"So is Larry letting vermin through?" I ask Lloyd in jest.

"He does, yeah," Lloyd deadpans. "Sorry Larry; the cat's out of the bag."

"That's right," laughs Larry. "It's always the fence down the road or the one up the road that let's them in."

I ask them what the main problems are and they answer in rapid-fire.

"Rain and wind pushing the sand around."

"Yeah, makes holes or builds it up."

"Pigs running straight through."

"They don't even stop."

"Do you ever see holes in the fence that you just can't work out?" I ask.

"You've usually got a rough idea," says Lloyd, looking to the more experienced Larry for embellishment.

"Usually the tracks give it away, whatever's gone through," Larry adds on cue.

"You've never found a hole without tracks?" I throw out there just for the rise. Lloyd picks it up without hesitation.

"There was a big hole up there once where Larry drove through when he nodded off one day," he says. "But everyone had a fair idea what it was."

We all laugh, and I suspect they'll both miss the banter and coffee at the Corner when Lloyd goes back to civilisation.

EUROPEAN CONNECTIONS

I'm reliably informed that the correct Polish pronunciation of Strzelecki is a straight-forward "Streletski". For some reason Australians insist on pronouncing each of the letters phonetically and the result is a more awkward effort most of us have to practice a few times before we get it right. Once or twice I've suggested to Australians that the Polish pronunciation might be the better option and been shouted down in flames. Perhaps, as one bloke suggested, "it came from what was slurred in the pub," and now it's *our* pronunciation, every bit as original as our version of Kosciuszko, the other famous Polish word we've butchered.

The Strzelecki Track was named by the explorer Charles Sturt in 1845 to honour the Polish explorer and geologist Sir Paul Edmund de Strzelecki, who is known to be the first European to climb Mt Kosciuszko. The Pole scaled Kosciuszko around 1840 during a geological survey of eastern Australia when he may or may not have been one of the first to discover gold in the Blue Mountains, depending on which history you believe. Either way, Strzelecki named the mountain after Polish national hero Tadeusz Kosciusko *(sic)*, who pronounced his name more along the lines of "Kozjooshka". All of which only goes to show that whoever discovered what where, Australian Polish is gold wherever you find it.

I think I was expecting too much from the Strzelecki. After hearing stories about it for years I'd built up expectations it could no longer meet. I knew about Harry Readford*, the cattle rustler who drove a herd of duffed** cattle from Queensland to South Australia via the Strzelecki Track, and then got pardoned by a jury in awe of his feat. I'd heard travellers speak of the Strezlecki in reverential tones, recalling diabolical breakdowns and long-term flood-ins. And I'd had fascinating conversations with truckies carting cattle to Queensland up the "Strez", quietly confident their enigmatic shrugs about road conditions meant far more than they were letting on. So over the years I'd allowed my imagination to create a barely-traversible goat track littered with fallen vehicles and a million stories.

Instead I got an A Grade dirt highway easily capable of transporting a conventional vehicle from one end to the other at top speed with nary a sideways glance at the landscape, which was featureless for the most part anyway. Admittedly my shortcut did join the Track below Merty Merty, where the Strzelecki Creek had cut the road, and the northern section does have more to offer a tourist including the Old Strzelecki Track. But as far as being an adventure road I was well off target, I daresay largely due to it now being the main access road to the Moomba Gas Fields.

I saw neither cattle nor pub nor any sign of a story on the Track, and made only the one camp; at Montecollina Bore. Now quite apart from being a pretty spot and a great place for a hot soak, I'd been told there were plenty of yabbies in the bore. But either I'd been sold a pup or I've lost my touch because I caught nothing. I resolved then and there to right the wrong and catch myself a feed

* Sometimes spelled Harry Redford, also known as Captain Starlight.
**Stolen

of yabbies before the trip was out or never eat crustaceans again!

Ridiculous promises aside, at the southern end of the Strzelecki Track is a story, albeit a tried and tested one. In fact I've already interviewed this man for radio and print*, but I thought I'd drop in on him again to commit him to video. His name is Talc Alf and in my opinion he's a national treasure. So please forgive my duplication.

Born in Holland and christened Cornelius Alferink, he came to Lyndhurst from Margaret River country some thirty-odd years ago and began carving talc, which was in good supply thereabouts at the time. These days he has an art gallery on the outskirts of town that he'll happily show you through if you have a notion to drop in. He's a generous and obliging soul and I've never known him to be less than hospitable, regardless of the hour or intention of your visit.

Though it's not his carvings that make Alf unique; it's his theories and postulations about everything from the origins of Aussie Rules football to why the swagman in Waltzing Matilda had a girlfriend with him when he was apprehended. He also has a truly original take on the etymology of our language and the meaning of words. For example he believes, among many other wonderful and even more fanciful derivations, that Australia means *east towards the golden sun*.

"When I was on my father's farm down in Margaret River," he explains, "I did think to myself at the time 'How come it's called the Golden West when everything's green?'

"Forty years later I'm here at Lyndhurst carving away and all of a sudden it dawned on me – and I should have worked it out a long

*In the first book, *Through Urban Eyes*.

time before because I've worked with geologists for years and I know the symbol for gold is *Au* – all of a sudden it hit me that was how the country got it's name: from Africa you're going towards the gold *Au* – the golden sunrise."

While not exactly a conventional explanation, there is a certain considered logic behind it, as there is with all his work. And I like this unstinting passion and confidence he has for his world view, and his willingness to share his ideas with whoever will listen. Before we even make our way into his gallery he uses a lump of talc to write the word *radio* on the side of a forty-four gallon drum, explaining to me how the *ra* comes from the sun and *dio* from God, and therefore it means the voice from God. I suspect he tells me this because he remembers my last visit and he's since given it some thought.

"*And*, look at this Monte, if you change the *ra* to *ro* you have *rodio* or rodeo as some people say, which means rolling with God on the back of a buckjumper, one minute you're alive and the next minute you could be dead with the buckjumper sitting on you." I've no idea why he tells me that but it makes me laugh.

It's a fine day in South Australia – as indeed most are – and once he's shown me the gallery Alf takes me on a tour of his property. He has a flowing grey beard and thick glasses beneath a floppy hat, and he chats freely as he shows me his concrete and talc block-making plant, his bicycle-powered washing machine and his unruly garden. He plucks a sweet potato leaf from one of the beds and offers me a taste, assuring me it's good to eat.

"It's like a salad," he adds.

I try the bitter green and hand it straight back to him. It's vile.

"No, I mean if you're going bad," Alf qualifies, picking at

another plant. "And this one here's a native leaf too, and when there's a lot of rain around it pops up everywhere. If you had a nice piece of kangaroo steak, some rice and *that*, you'd have yourself a good meal, wouldn't you?"

Again I try his offering, a succulent this time, and again I don't like it.

"Alf, it's awful! I'd have to be going really bad to eat that."

"Oh come on. This is all around. Like, Burke and Wills walked all across the country and came back to the waterhole at Innamincka and died, because they hadn't come to terms with the local conditions. They wouldn't listen to the blackfellas, see.

"And we're in the same position now," he continues. "We're not listening. It's not good enough. And if we don't listen we'll be in trouble one day."

"Let it go on record that Talc Alf is doing his bit."

"Bloody oath, I'm soldiering on for the land."

"But you can have as much of that stuff as you like," I say, pointing to the salad weed he's still holding. "Give me a good old-fashioned Iceberg lettuce, mate."

And we share a laugh but I know he thinks I'm a bit soft.

POPULATION ONE

When a town dies does the last to leave turn out the lights, or has that already been done?

Back in the 1980s Australian National ran the Transcontinental railway and every little town and siding along the Nullarbor Plain had life. Towns named after our Prime Ministers – like Barton, Deakin, Hughes and Cook – all played key roles along the line. Tarcoola in South Australia was a major player, providing services to both the east-west running Indian-Pacific and the north-south Ghan line to Alice Springs. Then in the 1990s Australian National transferred the responsibility for those lines to Australian Railtrack Corporation and withdrew its staff, and one by one the towns died. A woman who lived through Tarcoola's demise told me, "It happened slowly but then it happened. When I grew up here there were heaps of people. We had about sixty kids in school. But when the rail went private that's when the town closed, and it's like a ghost town now."

She's a young mother of three who's brought her family back to live in Tarcoola to help her own mother adjust to the recent loss of her husband. When I arrive she's supervising her two eldest kids in the schoolroom, but she tells me she feels they deserve a more challenging education now and the family is about to move back to the city, leaving her mother as the last permanent resident of the town.

"It must have been a comfort having your daughter and grand kids around through this?" I state the obvious to the older woman.

"It's been excellent, yeah," she nods. "I don't know how I would have coped otherwise."

"But now she's looking at going?"

"She has to for the children, you know. They need to be into a school."

And right on cue the youngest of the three boys interrupts us to clamber onto Grandma's lap and her face beams.

"This is my grandson," she introduces the squirming blonde lad as he nestles back against her.

I say hello to the boy and suggest she'll probably miss the kids.

"I will miss them, very much."

"I asked your daughter if she'll miss you and she said no." We both laugh.

This is one of those times I feel the privilege of my job. I've arrived in a remote location, completely unannounced, and invaded the private lives of a family. Initially they were a little wary, but somewhere along the way they remembered enjoying me doing the weather on the television and the doors opened. Now I'm being treated like an old family friend.

Earlier I walked the town to shoot overlay vision and saw the story in remnants. A weather board church in need of a coat of paint and a new roof. A dozen abandoned houses in various stages of disrepair. The old pub with a sign out front promising to re-open soon. Hot pink children's climbing bars in grounds being overrun by cactus. Jumbles of rusty trucks and assorted railway equipment next to what used to be sporting fields. You could almost see the order of evacuation.

"What's the most number of permanent residents you can remember here?"

"Oh, about a hundred-and-fifty people, could've been a little more. We had the hall, we had a shop, post office, school, police station, hospital...

"And they used to have cricket games, and soccer – way back there was enough to have four teams for soccer, two little teams and two older children's teams, and we used to have soccer every Saturday morning and cut up oranges to take over for half time, oh it was great, you know..."

I've never heard the act of cutting up oranges remembered so fondly before. I wonder if she can even bare to look at the sports ground now, with its sagging goalposts and rampant vegetation, some of it already the size of a man taking a position on the field. And because that kind of deterioration happens slowly does she see it as it is? Or as it was? Like a parent hardly notices the day-to-day growth in a child. I keep my thoughts to myself.

"And back then the train stopped twice a day so you could take a day trip to Port Augusta," she recalls with a smile. "Catch the train down in the morning and back that night."

"Do you miss that?"

"Oh, in a way, I suppose, but I'm happy here."

"Do you feel isolated?"

"No," she scoffs. "We've never felt isolated out here."

"Where does your mail come from?"

"Port Augusta. We've got a mailbox over at the old railway station; there's a big old red box there. They put it in there and we pick it up. Then on Thursdays we put our mail in the box and they take it away."

I saw the mailbox with the letters PMG stencilled on the door during my lap around town. Along with a solitary bench seat in the waiting room it appeared to be about the only working item at the station. While the building still appeared structurally sound the offices were junked, the windows broken and the doors hanging ajar. It didn't look like it was going to make old bones.

"Have they ever threatened to cut the power off?"

"Yes, several times. But I don't think they will."

It would probably be the death knell of the town if they did, but she reasons there's always workers around as well as her, presumably rail and communications gangs, perhaps even crews from the very electricity providers who would have her supply cut off. And who knows what long-term plans might be laid out for Tarcoola? The area is known to be rich in minerals and it is still the crossways between the two transcontinental rail lines. It's likely her quiet confidence is justified.

She's a gentle woman with strong eyes and greying hair, and she speaks with an air of calm resignation. Even when she's talking about the possibility of having her power cut off she shows no sign of anxiety or histrionics, only the occasional shrug of the shoulders or modest gesticulation with her hands. I notice her skin is very fine and clear for one who's lived most of her life in the desert, and she still wears her wedding band.

"So your late husband worked on the rail all his life?"

"Yes, he was a stationmaster and a station supervisor in later years, they renamed it. So it's been mainly railways all my married life, yeah."

She shows me a photo of him taken at the front of the station. He's a good-looking man with white hair and well-defined features in a tanned face, and he's looking away from the camera, probably up the line. I ask her if hearing the trains reminds her of her husband but she tells me she doesn't hear them.

"*Sometimes* I hear them," she corrects herself. "But even when I'm here at times by myself, you know, and I *do* hear them, it feels good, you know, comforting."

"I suppose if you do leave Tarcoola, a part of that leaving would feel as though you're leaving your husband?"

"Yeah. I've still got his ashes in the box but at the same time, yeah, I would. Because that's the only life I really knew. We were married when I was nineteen, you know. So it's been all railways and him, except for the last few years. So it will be hard, yeah."

DOWN THE LINE

As anticipated, the communication side of things hasn't been going well with my Big City Girl. Not for lack of opportunity or effort from my end, I hasten to add. As it happens my mobile service provider, while not one of Australia's most popular companies, does have excellent coverage in the bush, especially within about twenty kilometres of a town. So my *modus operandi* has been to camp on the outskirts of town, then begin the task of trying to make contact with her as I prepare dinner. Simple enough, you might think. But remember BCG doesn't actually answer her phone, doesn't even turn it on as a rule, for fear the people who provide the service she's no longer game to use, might have the audacity to expect payment for her previous usage.

"Why don't they stop annoying me?" she asked me once.

"Because they want you to pay your bill."

"Well I'd be more inclined to if they left me alone."

With logic like that they're bound to cut her some slack.

Anyway, so what we do is Skype. From the middle of the Australian bush to the suburbs of Sydney we Skype, laptop to laptop, face to face. And in spite of the occasional breakdown from ropey signals or whatever, it's a pretty reliable not to mention remarkable way to communicate at this time in history. No doubt in twenty, no, ten years it'll be rendered as obsolete as the carrier pigeon, but for now it serves us well.

Furthermore, we're playing some great venues. You see another wild thing about Skype is your set is wherever *you* are, so whenever there's enough light I'm outside proudly showing off the country.

"See those sheep grazing out there?" I direct the screen camera towards them. "They're dorpers. They shed their own fleece."

"Oh really, darling? What are they doing out of their cages?"

Of course being a product of the bustle and grind, the finer points of country life aren't really BCG's thing. And like most city folk she also takes technology for granted and adopts a very cavalier approach to the whole business; if she's around she'll accept my Skype request, if not she'll giggle an apology later.

All things considered, though, at least we have some form of contact and we still remember what each other looks like, if nothing else.

Surprisingly – to me at least – the best mobile coverage in remote Australia is along the Trans Australian Railway line. I could be wrong but there seems to be a tower every thirty kilometres or so, perhaps installed to give train travellers uninterrupted coverage across the Nullarbor Plain. Not a living soul within cooee, but rest assured they've got your mobile phone needs covered.

And it's an entertaining drive to boot. The road's a gentle roller coaster through some lovely mallee country and for the most part it's in reasonable nick, with plenty of railway history in the way of disused stops and sidings and the occasional train wreck along the way. I'm not much of a train nut myself, but I do remember being told the story of Ziggy, the Polish rail worker who built himself a shack out of railway sleepers at Mt Christie, then had to move it down the line to Barton when the train no longer stopped to drop his water and supplies. He moved the shack by hand, using only a wheelbarrow and a strong back to lug ten sleepers at a time, 50 kms along the track to his new location, then back for another load. Legend has it when he suffered a fall towards the end of his life and had to be taken in for medical treatment, the police had to shoot his dogs to gain access to him inside his shack. There's nothing so loyal as a good dog.

Water was always a problem along the line because there was no permanent supply. Indeed it was the ever-growing demand for water that led to the ultimate destruction of the Ooldea Soak. To quote Daisy Bates, writing of her sixteen years at Ooldea in *The Passing of the Aborigines*:

> *"In the few brief years since the white man's coming, 52 wells had been sunk, providing 70,000 gallons a week for the railway. The late H.Y.L. Brown, one of Australia's greatest pioneer geologists, had advised that no boring should be undertaken, but in continual experiment the blue clay-bed that formed a natural reservoir had apparently been pierced. The waters became brackish, injurious to the engines, unpleasant to the taste, and gradually seeped away. In October, 1926, Ooldea Soak closed down."*

Naturally this was a big setback for a steam railway, and thereafter all the holding tanks and reservoirs along the line had to be filled using supplies from either end of the sixteen hundred-odd kilometres of waterless track.

One such reservoir is at Wynbring, where the granite country briefly pushes up to the surface of the plain. It's a beautiful albeit improbable-looking waterhole cradled in an open fissure in the stone, like a huge granite bowl plonked in the middle of a vast paddock, with man-made rock walls offering containment where nature hasn't provided any. The only problem is the water's completely dead, stagnant to the last bunyip. Either from excessive salinity or just common or garden variety putrification I couldn't say, but these days there isn't a living thing goes anywhere near it.

Still it makes for a picturesque camp. And the communications tower within sight of the reservoir means we'll be able to Skype freely – read often enough so I'm almost guaranteed contact at least once during my overnight stay – and it occurs to me as I chat to my Big City Girl almost two thousand kilometres distant, watched by a ring of curious sheep edging ever closer to observe the odd spectacle of a man disgorged from a bus, communicating with some strange and wondrous creature living in a bright flickering thing on his lap, that in spite of the high level of technology we have at our disposal today, the gulf between the city and the bush was never wider.

MARALINGA RESORT

I'd wanted to shoot this story ever since I covered it for radio* a couple of years earlier: Maralinga – the tourist attraction. The concept had been tabled as a part of the business plan presented by the *Maralinga Tjarutja* people to the Federal Government leading up to the handover of *Section 400***** in 2009, and the prospect intrigued me.

Of course the grubby history of Maralinga is well-known in this country, but just to refresh your memory…

…back in the 1950s and 60s, with the complicity of the Menzies Government in Australia, the British Government set off a series of atomic explosions at Maralinga in the name of developing their nuclear capabilities. In the process the immediate environment was exposed to radioactive waste, and while cursory cleanups were undertaken by the British, most notably Operation Brumby in 1967, a Royal Commission in the 1980s determined the site was still contaminated to unacceptable levels. Consequently a second major cleanup was carried out in the 1990s, this time funded jointly by the Australian and British Governments. While this last rehabilitation program was said to meet "international best practice" standards at the time, there's been much debate over whether that was the case, indeed even what such standards are anyway, given this was the first nuclear cleanup of this magnitude anywhere in the world.

* For Charles Wooley's Across Australia programme in 2007, documented in **Red in the Centre**, *Through Urban Eyes*.

**The last piece of the Maralinga land to be classified Native Title and handed back.

Meanwhile, the human toll of the nuclear testing continues to be argued, lamented, refuted and disputed. What we do know, though, is that while efforts were made to clear the indigenous inhabitants from the area before testing began – a callous enough, though not unusual act for the times – there was no real appreciation for the nomadic nature of these people, or their inability to comprehend the warning signs erected at the testing sites. As a result many Aboriginal people were caught in the fallout, and this is not to forget or downplay the impact on the lives of thousands of civilians and service personnel who were effectively used as guinea pigs during the decade or so of testing at Maralinga. Indeed the ongoing ramifications are still being assessed, as second- and third-generation offspring of *all* people exposed to the testing exhibit genetic abnormalities at rates far exceeding the norm.

Yet these are matters for debate in courts of law and other forums more intellectually rigorous than these pages allow. My interest here is in the questions arising from the proposal of a tourist attraction on the old Maralinga site: Is it safe? What's there for people to see? And is there enough interest in nuclear tourism to justify the proposal, or is it just lip service?

Maralinga is located in the Great Victoria Desert region of South Australia, about 200 kilometres north of Yalata on the Eyre Highway. The landscape is mainly mallee and saltbush scrub over stony, reddish soil, presenting the driver with a monotony of ageless green stretching to the horizon. There are no hills to speak of, nothing to break ranks and draw the eye, and when the wind blows from the Southern Ocean even the beetles take refuge.

Approaching from the south – the northern access from Emu is now closed due to its proximity to sacred sites – the first thing you'll notice as you near the base is a radical improvement in the quality of the road; without warning the dirt suddenly becomes bitumen, giving the distinct impression you're heading somewhere significant, which you surely are.

The next incongruity you'll see is *The Tardis* phone booth at the front gates. A pale blue concrete cylinder complete with painted-on windows outside and directions where to stand inside – "Put 'em feet" – *The Tardis* houses the old Bakelite wind-up telephone used by visitors to notify the base of their arrival. It's a whimsical touch to such a significant check point, though the rough-welded signature plate assures me it was built well after the testing ceased. After all, one can hardly imagine the stuffy British 'brass' tolerating such frivolity.

I crank my call to the caretaker and he duly arrives in his utility, radio blaring and somewhat distracted because he's listening to the footy. "I took Essendon this week," he tells me with a laugh, "in the tipping competition. 'Cause they're playing at home, you know?"

He unlocks and opens the gates and we shake hands. He's a gruff-looking man wearing an old cap and a face full of stubble, and he speaks in a gravelly, faraway voice that sounds slightly manufactured, like he's broadcasting 'off mike'. In contrast his manner is engaging and friendly, and when we reach the village he's apologetic asking if I mind him hearing out the game before he shows me around. I make no objection and give myself a quick tour while I wait.

In its day the Maralinga village accommodated thousands

of British, Australian and New Zealand defence personnel, all directly or indirectly involved in the nuclear experiments. No expense was spared to make the living conditions as comfortable as possible, and as well as the usual array of quarters and mess halls and even a hospital, they had a full size Olympic pool, a cinema showing the latest movie releases and sporting facilities to rival most country towns, including a nine hole golf course hewn out of the unforgiving scrub. Speaking a few days earlier with an engineer who served there through the early sixties, the impression I got was that there were few cushier postings at the time than Maralinga.

"It was regarded then by everybody there," he told me, "that you were the elite, the top end of Defence.

"In England we got seven shillings and tuppence a day to feed one man, for all his meals," he continued, "over at Maralinga we got a pound*. A cold collation was half crayfish, whole schnapper, help yourself to everything, you know. Or you could have T-bone steaks and topsides, all the veges, roasts, the choice of meals was incredible.

"As far as army life goes," he concluded, "compared to the Pommy stuff you get in Europe, up there was paradise, you know, brilliant. Yeah, I enjoyed my time up there."

These days, though, it's hard to imagine the village was once at the cutting edge of military research. Many of the twenty or so corrugated iron buildings are showing signs of neglect, the pool has been filled with dirt (*Pit 68U*) and looks like a partly excavated Roman ruin, and the sporting fields are being taken over by the natural order. Only the hospital – now used as living quarters by

---

*About three times as much in the old money.

the caretaker and his family – and a handful of facilities sheds look well-maintained, and the water tower, I'm pleased to report because I climbed it with camera and tripod under-wing, is still sturdy.

A door to one of the khaki buildings stands slightly ajar so I enter. It looks like it was an office of some kind judging by its contents, or maybe a laboratory, and it has the dishevelled air of a room abandoned in a hurry. There are opened cardboard boxes strewn over desks and tables, roller chairs pushed into corners, plastic buckets and liquid chemical containers on shelves against the walls, and a couple of sinks and a gas bottle, all of it wearing a telltale frosting of red desert dust. Here and there a hastily scribbled signature on a door or wall gives evidence of previous visitors, and a couple of the three-winged radiation warnings and Commonwealth of Australia Prohibited Area signs remind me of where I am. On the door to a room off the main area is a handwritten sign saying: *The equipment in this room belongs to the <u>Australian Radiation Laboratory</u>. Some of it is contaminated. Do not touch!* Inside I find a bench press and exercise bicycle where someone has set up a makeshift gym.

Footy game over, the caretaker gives me the Cook's tour of the grounds. *En route* he points out a number of heritage listed buildings and the enormous generator plant, and I imagine the maintenance costs for the place wouldn't be small. Some estimates I've seen put the figure at around a quarter of a million dollars a year, and taking the caretaker's package into account it's not a difficult number to believe.

The airport, too, would require maintaining if tourists were to be flown in. When I interviewed the Maralinga Tjarutja General Manager for radio back in 2007, he outlined a vision that included whale watching in the Bight as part of a total Nullarbor/ Maralinga experience, and fanciful or not there's little doubt Maralinga could handle the traffic. At 3.5 kilometres in length the bitumised airstrip could easily land an Airbus full of sightseers, if it came to that.

On the way into the terminal we cross the infamous Bridge of Sighs, where arriving servicemen would express their displeasure at the desolate surroundings, while those leaving would also sigh, though reflecting something more like "Thank Christ that's over". Oleanders imported from the Old Country and planted along the walkway would doubtless have heightened the sentiments.

The terminal is empty of all but a few drums and barrels and a latish model 4WD with a wooden front door hatch, obviously customised to perform some sort of nuclear dirty work. The caretaker tells me it was used during the second cleanup to take scientists into the Forward Area to identify the hot spots, or areas where plutonium could still be detected. It looks a bit slap-dash to my untrained eye, like something out of a movie where everyone wears white overalls and gas masks; which probably wasn't far from the truth, except only the whitefellas got protection in this story – according to anecdotal evidence the blackfellas were not given protection.

Next morning we drive to the Forward Area where the nuclear explosions were detonated. It's a surreal experience travelling in the pink and blue dawn, headlights arresting the shrubs growing on the road like rabbits frozen in the glare, heading to the scene of Australia's most cynical hour.

By the time we reach Taranaki the sun is crowning and I can see what Len Beadell saw in the site. "We all knew immediately that this was to be the place," the man employed by the military to find the location wrote later in one of his books. "We solemnly wrung each other's hands and just gazed about us in all directions for half an hour." Indeed the saltbush plain does seem to stretch on forever, with only the Taranaki plinth and the waste pit rising above the knee-high vegetation.

"Taranaki was the biggest atomic weapon that was ever let loose out here," the caretaker tells me, "and it was twenty-seven kiloton, equivalent to twenty-seven thousand tons of TNT. The plinth was put here by the British after the cleanup in 1967."

The plinth is a concrete pyramid with its top cut off, standing about two metres high. On one face is the proclamation *TEST SITE TARANAKI A BRITISH ATOMIC WEAPON WAS TEST EXPLODED HERE ON 9 OCT 1957,* and on another the eerily prescient statement *RADIATION LEVELS FOR A FEW HUNDRED METRES AROUND THIS POINT MAY BE ABOVE THOSE CONSIDERED SAFE FOR PERMANENT OCCUPATION.*

"It's almost as if they knew their cleanup was rubbish," I suggest.

"Yes, they did not clean it up properly," the caretaker nods, "and that's why they had to come back and do the major cleanup in 1996."

"So that's the last cleanup pile there?"

"Correct, that's what we call the Taranaki burial pit. It's approximately fifteen metres deep, and it contains three hundred and thirty thousand cubic metres of plutonium-contaminated earth from this two square kilometre site here, that they reburied over there and put clean fill on top of it."

What we're looking at is an area of raised dirt roughly the size of half a dozen football fields, flattened on top like a man-made mesa, with the natural vegetation slowly re-establishing. At the head of the pile is a sign warning of what's buried within, bearing a *No Camping* icon with *NGURU WIYA* written underneath, words I assume reinforce the point for speakers of the two dominant languages of the region *Pitjantjatjara* and *Yankunytjatjara*.

"So you're quite confident the site's clean now?"

"Very, very confident," the caretaker assures me. "We've spoken to a lot of the scientists who've been out here, and everybody has said that the only hazard at Taranaki right now is if you trip over one of these big rocks and break your ankle."

Indeed many scientists *have* declared the Taranaki site clean, although as alluded to in the opening paragraphs there've been serious doubts expressed about the integrity of the final cleanup, to the point where some experts are now saying it won't be the last. And while the caretaker is effectively backing his beliefs with his own life, there are contradictions.

At the base of the plinth at the Breakaway site – there's a plinth at each of the seven major test sites – he draws my attention to a piece of pale green rock, so naturally I reach down to collect it.

"Don't pick it up!" he warns, making me almost shit myself before he picks the rock up himself using his handkerchief. "When they let the tower blast off here it vaporised everything in the area for around four hundred metres, and turned the ground to molten glass. It's been cleaned up, but there are still a few pieces left."

"So is that radio-active?"

"It's mildly radio-active," he admits. "If you broke that apart, there's tiny air bubbles in there with slightly radio-active dust inside."

It's probably not life-threatening, but the shock brings me back to earth. If there is still known radio-active waste lying about on the ground, who's to say there aren't more hot spots likely to surface in years to come that we don't know about? From my research it appears the British supplied highly questionable records of what was buried where, and clearly the last cleanup didn't get it all. And let's not forget we're talking about something with a half life of around a quarter of a million years; a warning sign will be lucky to last the first hundred! And if we're not sure where it all is now, how are we going to keep track of it down through the ages? If nothing else it surely highlights just how environmentally irresponsible the whole exercise was in the first place.

For the rest of the morning we visit some of the other test sites and points of interest. At the Marcoo crater site I'm told the story of the Milpuddie family, who were found living in the crater made by the explosion because rabbits blinded by the blast were easy to catch and rain collected in the crater provided a ready supply of water.

"Did they survive?"

"The old girl passed away recently from old age," the caretaker answers me. "But her grandchildren have got birth deformities; we believe it's gone down through the genes."

In fact the Milpuddie family have suffered many health problems since the exposure to radiation, including a number of still-born babies, but the authorities continue to deny any connection. Although as well as the *No Camping* signs there are now also signs with a kangaroo icon and the words KUKA PALYA; again I can only assume this is a *Pitjantjatjara/Yankunytjatjara* warning.

Curiously the native animals have yet to return to the Maralinga site in any numbers. It's on record that the plains were teeming with wildlife before the nuclear explosions, yet since then only the introduced animals seem to have accepted the post-nuclear landscape. As the caretaker says, "It's just like this is still a dead zone." In my time there I saw not one kangaroo, not one Plains Turkey, and heard not one bird call. I did see a small herd of camels, though, adding further support to the caretaker's theory that only the native animals boycotted the site.

But perhaps the best example of the cavalier nature of the testing is left till the last of my tour. Standing at the ready beside one of the sites prepared but never used for the eighth detonation, are about fifty rusty contraptions the like of which I've never seen before. About a metre and a half in height, they look like oversized caulking guns on legs. They are, I'm told, smoke rocket launchers.

"They were designed to be set up fifty metres apart," the caretaker explains, "and when the mushroom cloud first started forming as the bomb went off, these were ignited and shot through the cloud to give an idea of wind direction, to see if the cloud was still travelling in the direction it was supposed to be going."

"And if it wasn't?"

"I couldn't answer that question."

"Did they go out and catch it in a bag and bring it back?"

It's a light moment but one not without its sinister truth; the smoke rockets were designed, like the rest of the Maralinga experiments, for bloody-minded scientific research alone; where the fallout went was of little concern to the British. To their mind the welfare of the Aborigines (or any other Australians, for that matter) was the responsibility of the Australian Government. Indeed to this point the British have shown a grim reluctance to accept responsibility for even their own Maralinga-affected personnel, prompting some commentators to speculate that they're simply waiting till they all die so there'll be no need for compensation.

I ask the caretaker his thoughts on the tourism proposal.

"I think, myself, the tourism idea is good. What they're going to do, the Maralinga Tjarutja people, is leave the whole area for a period of healing, maybe twelve months to two years, and in that period of time explore the avenues of setting a tourism enterprise up out here. And the potential here is huge; everybody wants to come out and see the Maralinga bomb sites, and especially the Taranaki site. Then there's the village with six heritage listed sites, the old hospital in pristine condition, a couple of the old bedding stores, footy ovals…"

"Do you think there's enough interest in nuclear tourism out there?"

"There is. Last year we had over five hundred people come through the village, with a lot of tourists who were very interested because they could remember the bombs going off or had relations who worked out here, and a lot of young people who came out with their parents, who had no previous idea about the history, but left wanting to research it for themselves."

Indeed while *I* was researching this chapter I came across half a dozen websites dedicated solely to nuclear tourism, and any number of travel articles from countries as diverse as the USA, China, Japan, Kazakhstan and the Marshall Islands about one of the fastest-growing sectors of the adventure tourism industry. Under such witty titles as *Nuclear Tourism: It's Hot* (World Hum) and *Chernobyl Gets Glowing Reviews* (The Times) we learn that there's no shortage of people queueing up to visit any number of nuclear sites around the world. There's even a newly-released book called *A Nuclear Family Holiday* written by a couple of journalists (Hodge

& Weinberger) who expose the covert world of atomic weaponry under the loose assertion that, to quote them quoting fellow author Tom Vanderbilt, "all wars end in tourism".

"How do you rate this chapter in Australia's history?" I ask the caretaker.

"Myself, I rate it as a terrible chapter. I don't think it should have happened, but nobody knew what was going to happen back then. But I believe this place here should never change the way it is now. It is history; it's indigenous history, it's Australian history and it's British and world history here, and it should stay exactly the same."

But not everyone sees the obvious as the most important factor in the equation. Oak Valley is the community set up to accommodate the displaced Maralinga Tjarutja people who wanted to return to their country. I talk with a man from Oak Valley who also sits on the Maralinga Tjarutja board, about the plans for the site. He's an articulate man who speaks with objectivity and restraint, but he's clearly passionate about the topic and believes both sides of the story aren't yet being given equal weight.

"I think we're slightly getting away from the whole reason of getting that land back," he says. "It was supposed to be set up as a Land Management Heritage Resource Centre, to be run by the local Aboriginal people."

"Do you think it's getting hijacked by the tourism talk?"

"Yeah, I mean let's not rule it out, use it as a drawcard if you like, to bring the people to this region. But remember that region is also very sensitive and sacred to local Aboriginal people, and they've got to have control of that Section 400. At the moment you've got whitefellas, non-Aboriginal people, taking tourists in there and all they're doing is talking about the bomb testing.

"There's a whitefella story there," he continues, "and there's a blackfella story just as important. You've only got to look at this country; you've got whitefella story on top, but underneath it you've got blackfella story, and it's a bit unfortunate that this region is one of those places."

So, I'll see you at the opening, then?

Footnote: At the time of writing discussions had begun between the Maralinga Tjarutja and the British Government, to seek a contribution to help restore and maintain this significant piece of British history. The Australian Federal Government has already contributed six million dollars towards the upkeep of the village.

TIETKINS WELL

As an interesting aside to the last story, Maralinga very nearly didn't happen. Or at least not on the current site. In1874, back when the land was still referred to as "north of the Ooldea ranges", explorer Ernest Giles passed through with his trusty lieutenant William Tietkens. At the time the land was at its best, with wildlife in abundance and the plains covered in spear grass as tall as a man and great stands of blue bush and saltbush everywhere. This particularly impressed Tietkens, who applied for a pastoral lease over the land upon his return to Adelaide. The lease was granted on the proviso that he could find water and show the land's viablility, so he advertised for a couple of well-diggers to do the job. But finding them proved more difficult than he imagined, and after eighteen months and any number of potential starters reneging once they saw the harshness of the country, Tietkens had to resort to a more innovative approach.

"So he got two Russian sailors off a sealing ship," the caretaker continues, "got 'em drunk down at Fowlers Bay, Shanghai-ed 'em, kept 'em drunk all the way up here to what we now call Tietken's Plain, and told them to dig him a well.

"He left them with a hogshead of water, a rifle, some salted meat, and enough alcohol to keep them drunk for seven days so that when they did sober up they wouldn't have known where to go back to. So they had to sit there and dig the well. And they did. They stayed nine months here and dug the well."

"And found no water?"

"And found no water."

The well is twenty-six metres deep and roughly two metres by one in dimension, with the upper five metres of the drop reinforced with timber ribbing. Below that the soil looks stony and unforgiving, and one can only feel for the two Russians breaking their backs on such a fruitless exercise.

"Poor buggers." I look around and try to imagine what they'd have felt being dumped out here. It may have looked lush to Tietkens once, but today it looks barren and hostile, no place to be if you're fresh off the boat. Quite apart from the heat, they'd have had to contend with flies, snakes, scorpions, dingoes and of course the local Anangu people who we know from Giles' records showed hostility towards the white man. Never mind the psychological challenge of not knowing where they were, what they'd use for transport even if they did, and what would happen to them if Tietkens never returned.

"What did they live in?"

"He left them with a big sheet of canvass and they cut a few trees down and pitched a bush tent over there in that stand of trees," he points to a spot about a hundred metres distant where a few upright posts still mark the corners of their shelter. The white-anted remains of their camp beds lay collapsed on the ground, and interestingly, a stack of firewood sits untouched off to one side; waiting a hundred and thirty years for a fire that never got lit, by two men waiting nine months for a wage that never got paid. For when Tietkens returned he was so disgusted with their efforts that he told them they were lazy and refused to pay.

Not to be denied so easily, when Tietkens dropped the Russians off he Shanghai-ed another two sailors and had them dig a second well three kilometres to the south of well number one. This time they did strike water, but of such poor quality it was unfit even for stock to drink. It's not known whether he paid these well-diggers, though he did give up looking for water after that.

"And if he had gone six kays up the road to the north," the caretaker continues, "and sunk it in a natural depression where Lenny Beadell put one in '54, he would've come on fresh water – which they call Fresh Bore now – this would've been a pastoral lease, and Maralinga would not have been here."

And the little irony in this is, Maralinga only happened in the fist place because the British wanted to compete in the nuclear arms race with America and Russia. So had Tietkens been a little smarter with his choice of location, the Russians might have knocked Britain out of the race a hundred years sooner.

THE SPINIFEX EXPERIENCE

Driving west from Maralinga I come across a car on the side of the road so I pull up to see if they need help. At first glance I can't tell how many people have spilled out, but it's more than four and less than ten. Some are sitting by the fire they've lit, others are hanging beside the car and one woman has bright orange hair that my eyes refuse to leave or believe. I can't say for sure if there are any babies but I can vouch for at least a couple of dogs. If it's not the whole catastrophe it'll do until the real thing turns up.

I jump out of the cabin and a man I assume to be the driver approaches me and says, in perfect English, "Goonunnanay drath?"

I say, "What?"

"Drath, drath," he repeats, "Goonunnanay drath?"

He's a man of about thirty years with a humourless face who's soon joined by an older man with grey hair and a wad of chewing tobacco in the corner of his mouth. Together they repeat the first man's utterings as if by turning up the volume its meaning will become clearer to me. Then the older man starts gesticulating at the back of their car with his walking stick, and after a few false leads it dawns on me he's pointing to the gas nozzle and they're asking if I've got any gas.

I say no and ask where they're going. And if I hadn't previously heard the name, wasn't already going there myself and knew it was the only community within cooee, I wouldn't have had a clue what they said. But their destination was Oak Valley.

Then the woman with bright orange hair comes up and asks if I've got water, and she's so much easier to understand than the men I fancy she can do the interpreting, except that shock of hair she's wearing would be too distracting. I'm told later the unfortunate happenstance is the result of trying to dye grey hair red, but she looks too young for grey hair and it might be more like the effect Japanese surfers get when they try to dye black hair blonde. Only this is even louder if you can imagine that, almost to the volume of a fluoro safety vest. I give her water with my eyes averted.

Then she asks if I've got sandwiches, and it's probably not the most unusual request I've had in the middle of the desert, but again it'll do for now. I say no, I'm right out of sandwiches, have you got any rope? She looks at me like I'm a moron, as if she thinks I'm offering her rope to eat instead of a sandwich. I let her think what she wants and ask the men the same question. But of course a carload of people with no water or food and not enough gas to get home doesn't have rope, so I unpack the snatch strap and hitch them up for a tow.

"Slowly, slowly," the orange one urges as they all pile into their car and I head for the cabin. "You go slow one, okay?"

"Yeah, yeah, I'll go slow. Just don't hit your brakes or your tow bar'll pull straight off."

So off we set, into the western sun, a bright red and blue bus towing a carload of orange and black.

I get Claude up to about seventy and maintain that speed. He seems comfortable there. Indeed if I didn't know him better I'd think he was almost enjoying the task. But apparently my passengers aren't enjoying it nearly as much and after about ten kilometres I see the driver's arm come out the window, and though his signal isn't clear I figure he isn't trying to improve on his tan so I pull up.

"What's up?"

"You go slowly, Monte." It's Orange again. It seems she's assumed the role of interpreter anyway. "People very frightened in here."

"I'm only doing seventy."

"You go maybe forty, better."

"Forty? Too slow. We'll be driving in the dark. Sixty."

So we agree on fifty-five and off we set again, me not quite believing I've just capitulated to a mob of people I'm doing a favour.

A little further on it occurs to me I should get a shot of this for the travelogue and pull over again. With the camera over my shoulder I walk back and explain that I'm just going to get a passing shot of the two cars under tow because that's my job, then walk a hundred yards ahead to set up the shot. Camera rolling I walk back to see the arm out the window again.

"What's up this time?"

"Dat camera dere?" It's the driver.

"Yeah, I told you what I was doing."

"You can't take pictures of Aboriginal people. It's illegal." Suddenly he speaks flawless English.

So there'll be no filming. There's no point trying to explain the shot's so wide you'd be lucky to make out the orange beacon let alone any facial features. Now my hitchhikers are not only controlling my speed but restricting my work as well. To be honest my patience is starting to wear thin.

Then about fifty kilometres from Oak Valley I pull over to take

THE UPRISING
Above: S*unrise, Montecollina Bore, SA* (story page 28)
Below: *Moonrise, Montecollina Bore, SA*

THE LEGEND

_____ The Trip

— · — · — · — State Borders

THE STATS

Vehicle: "Claude" 4WD Hino Bus
(aka BB58 Toyota Coaster)

Kilometres: Approx. 30,000

Time: 5 months

Repairs: Response unprintable

Summary: Claude almost killed me

Map is representative only

THE LOW LIFE
Above: *Conspicuous Camouflage, Bing Bong, NT*
Below: *Desert Shade, via Tibooburra, NSW*

THE HIGH LIFE
Above: *Boab Strainer, Kimberley, WA*
Below: *Textured Trunk, North QLD*

THE CHEEKY
Top left: *"Glenora" & Kyra, Karumba, QLD* (story page 213)
Top right: *The Wild Bunch, QLD*
Bottom left: *Give Way to Crocodiles, Cahill's Crossing, NT* (story page 134)
Bottom right: *Shutup and make like a coconut, Karumba, NT*

THE UNFORGETTABLE (story page 43)
Above: *The Tardis, Maralinga, SA*
Below: *Smoke Rocket Launchers, Maralinga, SA*

THE INDUSTRIOUS
Top left: *Post Modern, Timber Creek, NT*
Top right: *Pipe Man, Stuart Highway, NT*
Bottom left: *Change of Plan, Mataranka, NT*
Bottom right: *Defenseless, Chillagoe, QLD*

a snapshot of a *Lift em foot** sign at the roadside and discover my stills camera is missing. I must have left it at Maralinga. I'll have to unhitch my passengers and go back to get it.

"I've left my camera** at Maralinga," I tell the driver. "Have to go back." I begin uncoupling the tow strap.

"You leave us here?"

"Pick you up on the way back."

"No, no, you take us Oak Valley first, then go back Maralinga after."

"No, you wait here. I'll leave you water and food and you might get another lift in the meantime."

Then they're all out of the car pointing and jabbering at me and none of it's pretty, and I'll spare you a transcript but they threw everything at me from emotional blackmail to character assassination. Violence even looked possible at one point. In the end I relented and towed them into the community. But not content with that, then they wanted me to tow them around town while they looked for what I never did figure out. At one stage wanting me to turn so sharply on the tow rope we'd have wiped out trees with their car, at another sending the old man up front to guide me to wherever the hell it was we were going. But he seemed to have less idea than me so I ended up unhitching them nowhere in particular and leaving them to their own devices. The last words I heard were Orange saying, "I can travel with you?" I didn't look, didn't even turn around, just drove away.

---

* Aboriginal term for "slow down", usually painted on an old car bonnet or a 44 gallon drum placed at the roadside.

Generously delivered the next day by a **Commercial Helicopters pilot who diverted his charter for Iluka Mining Company to do so.

I was a guest of the community for a night and a day and several times saw my hitchhikers, who showed no sign of recognition. Only once was there any acknowledgement, and that was when the old man learned I'd given another old man some money for a story. "That other old man only a boy," he told me in a confidential tone. "I'm a man. Next time you bring money, we talk. I tell you good story. If you like, then you pay." Again I was amazed at how the English improved when it really mattered. Not to mention the insightful reference to paying only if I liked the story: in a comedy of errors the old bloke I had offered to pay refused to go on camera, and then still insisted on being paid for some rubbish story he told me off-camera that I had no use for, and for the second time in twenty-four hours I was obliged to compromise to avoid hostility. So I gave him twenty dollars, and the second old man – my tobacco-chewing hitchhiker – must have heard about this and figured there'd be a quid in it for him if he told me what I wanted to hear. I've no doubt they both figured I was a soft touch.

At some point during my stay I told the towing story to one of the community workers I met. "Welcome to the Spinifex Experience," came the understanding reply.

PILA NGURU

I spent a week in Spinifex Country and loved it. I loved the desert plains covered in spinifex bush and mallee trees reaching their short arms up to the irresistible blue. And I loved the red sandhills dotted with Desert Oak and saltbush and samphire rolling between little sandstone gullies and washaways. And I especially loved the warmth of the desert people, the Spinifex People.

Oak Valley is a small community about a hundred kilometres to the north west of Maralinga. It was set up to give the displaced some homeland to go to when the Maralinga Tjarutja land* was returned to its traditional owners in 1985, although it wasn't settled as a community for another decade after that. The people came mainly from Yalata, a mission two hundred and fifty kilometres to the south on the Eyre Highway. Forty years previously Yalata had been established by the Lutheran Church to take the Maralinga and Ooldea Soak Aboriginals relocated before the testing began. However, trying to throw a blanket of origin over these highly nomadic people is a sure way to do your head in. Described variously as *Pitjantjatjara, Yankunytjatjara, Ngaanyatjara, Maralinga Tjarutja, Anangu* and almost every conceivable combination of the above, I'm never entirely sure whether the reference is to a language, region or people, or indeed whether the description is coming from someone as clueless as me. Conveniently, though, right throughout this region they also consider themselves Spinifex

*With the exception of Section 400.

People, or *Pila Nguru**, so for the sake of clarity (not to mention my own sanity) I'll run with that.

It's true I was hoping to find someone at Oak Valley prepared to talk about Maralinga, but mostly my leads were unable, unwilling or unaffordable, so I changed tack. I decided to follow the music instead. I'd made a loose arrangement with Australia Network to keep an eye out for musical stories for their new art show, Highlights, and this seemed like a good place to start. Before I left I had a notion to explore the musical undercurrent of outback Australia. For some reason I thought we might have our own sly version of the American Deep South scene, or some Ozark-style hillbilly tonk out there somewhere just waiting to be discovered. I don't know, maybe I took too many drugs when I was younger, but naively I imagined bizarre home-made instruments in rainforest communes, grappa-fuelled squeezebox sessions at the opal mines and maverick maestros plying their trade to unappreciative snot-nosed kids in back country hovels. It didn't take long to work out I was dreaming, looking for the H Chord again. That ideal doesn't exist, at least not in any significant way in white man's Australia. There are strong signs of it, however, in Aboriginal Australia.

There's a lot one can say about blackfella communities but you can't deny they've got a musical pulse. Whatever far-flung outpost you find yourself in you'll hear music somewhere in the mix. It's as ubiquitous as the howling of dogs and the awful din of domestic disenchantment; that driving beat and lonesome guitar. They suck it up from an early age and take it with them for the ride. As one Oak

---

*From Scott Cane's authoritative book **Pila Nguru**, "They call themselves, if anything, the *Anangu tjuta pila nguru* – meaning the Aboriginal people (*Anangu*) many (*tjuta*) spinifex (*pila*) from (*nguru*)."

Valley man told me, it's a natural extension of their storytelling.

"Music's always in Aboriginal culture because that's how we tell stories, too; through the singing of corroboree songs. It's an important thing, not only in Aboriginal communities but all communities.

"When I came here in 1997 there was no band. And I was sitting outside here one night and I could hear some music up at the community there. So I go up and have a look and it's a couple of blokes sitting around playing guitars, couple of rusty old microphones and battered up amplifiers and stuff, and they were singing all this country gospel stuff in the local language. And it sounded really good. So I said, well I've got a guitar and a bit of gear as well, do you mind if we have a go tomorrow night? And it just built on from there."

It sounds easy, but don't be fooled.

"The thing is, music brings people together," he explains. "But in a community like this it brings everything together including the bloody dogs. So you've got to separate the amplifiers and the instruments from the dogs and everything else. And just organising everybody, you know, keeping them on time. Us blackfellas we just go from sunup to sundown, there's no midday or morning tea or whatever. 'What time you going to get out of bed?' And he might point straight up top here. Oh, that's midday, yeah.

"And there's none of this balancing, you know, no equalizers," he continues, "It's more like 'I want to turn mine up loud, I want everyone to hear me', you know? So everyone does.

"And by the time the night's out, we might go down with five fellas in the band, but there's other family members that go along and say, 'I want to get up and have a play too', so by the time the night's out you've probably gone through about half a dozen drummers, and the same with guitarists, you know?"

He's likable ambassador for his community and his people, and he makes me laugh at the vagaries of being in an Aboriginal band. But his attitude is more serious when it comes to the dispossession of Aboriginal land at Maralinga.

"You take the people away from their country they got no culture they got no law. Only law they got is the whitefella's law out there, and we can't think whitefella's law. We get to learn it because we're locked up all the time for not doing things the whitefella way. All we want is the whitefella to understand a bit about our culture."

He plays me a song he's written on the subject, called Spinifex Man:

> *'Spinifex Man, Spinifex Man, proud of his people*
> *and proud of his land,*
> *The desert people, the desert land, all belong to*
> *that Spinifex Man.'**

"And that's for all the Spinifex People," he concludes, "the people of this region."

And I guess I get my Oak Valley perspective, after all.

My next spinifex stop is Tjuntjuntjara, another community established for the Maralinga displaced. Tjuntjuntjara is over the border in Western Australia and to drive from Oak Valley I need another permit, which is graciously supplied at short notice and personally delivered to my roadside camp by a member of the Council. As it happens he was travelling east with his family

---

*Chorus from *Spinifex Man*, reproduced with thanks to Chris Dodd.

as I was going west, but it remains to this day the most positive experience I've ever had with Aboriginal bureaucracy.

At Tjuntjuntjara I visit the school and play the kids a song. Before long the music shed is opened up and the big kids are summonsed and the afternoon evolves into an all-in jam session, with little kids drumming along on garbage tins and buckets and girls dancing on makeshift stages and, yes, even the dogs getting amongst the action; again the music takes over, and I'm pretty sure I hear a few H chords in there too.

The headmistress is refreshingly accepting. "That's the way we operate," she smiles. "Amongst that we've got important objectives that we achieve, but flexibility is the absolute key. And we've got to be prepared to grab any opportunity that could be educational for the kids, because we're so isolated. We're so focussed on literacy and numeracy, which are important, but we sometimes forget that these kids have other talents that we need to nurture.

"And those older kids, they love their music, it's a big motivator. So they'll come into school and do activities with the little tackers, or take them for footy training after school, because they know that the trade-off is we'll welcome them in to play music."

She's a woman of easy bearing who shines with the look of contentment you only find on people doing what they want to be doing. She's constantly interacting with the kids and it's clear they warm to her. As we speak she has one of the younger boys sitting contentedly on her lap, and I'm reminded that teachers used to do this all the time, before it was forbidden. She tells me she was fed up with teaching and took some long service leave to travel, and just happened to be passing through when she was offered the position. She was unsure, but agreed to try it out and fell in love with the kids, the people and the desert.

"They're just so welcoming," she gushes. "It's very easy to fit in and feel like part of the community, here. It can take a while for people to get to know you, to know you're not another Toyota Person…"

"A blow-in?"

"Yeah. Toyota People. They wear out and go away and you get another one," she laughs. "But once they know you're here for the right reasons… I mean, we've been asked to go out dancing in the bush with people, women's ceremony business, and that was just a fantastic experience. We went out there, and it was mothers daughters, grandmothers, aunties, nieces, all dancing together around a fire under the moon, and it was just like, to me the most amazing experience. And to be invited to be part of that was incredible. I know at the time I said to the other teachers 'I've been to the Taj Mahal, and I've been to The Pyramids and The Great Wall of China but this easily ranks up there with them'. Because it was just such a magic, beautiful night."

"So has all this given you a renewed enthusiasm for teaching?"

"Absolutely has. Just working with these kids. They're completely unspoilt. In fact, when I first came here I taught them frisbee. And I used to try and put them into two even teams. And I'd notice that after a while if one team was winning, the teams would change, without a word being spoken. And what they were doing is kids were melding into one team or the other to keep the scores even. Because that's the way you live; you look after everybody, you don't just look after yourself."

I leave Tjuntjuntjara wishing they were all like that, but knowing that's definitely an ideal that doesn't exist. One of the main reasons communities like Tjuntjuntjara can operate well is because they're dry, no alcohol, and their remoteness actually works in their favour. As a simple rule the further away – geographically, culturally, *essentially* – from civilisation the better chance a community seems to have of holding onto its cultural integrity. But how do you reconcile that with modern Australia, with urbanisation and capitalism and even democracy, for Christ's sake?

I move on, heading north to Ulkurlka. I wanted to see the smart, new community roadhouse/store built from Maralinga Tjaritja compensation funds. And I'd also heard about the Department of Environment and Conservation project underway up there, where desert wildlife was being trapped and catalogued by scientists, then presented to the local elders for identification so a cross-cultural glossary could be established.

So it was with a real sense of anticipation that I headed up the track from Tjuntjuntjara. I'd been warned the sandhills grew in stature the further north one travelled, and also that the boss from Ilkurlka would be travelling down the road to catch a plane the next morning. So I made camp about halfway along on a stretch where I'd get a good view of his vehicle approaching the next day, rather than risk meeting him on the crest of a sandhill.

Camping in the desert is like no other experience. To begin with there's almost always some kind of breeze moving through the trees, giving a sense of company. Then there are the colours: the rust red sandhills; the many greens of the foliage from silver through lime to olive and khaki; and of course the rude blue of the sky giving way to the scene-stealing stars as the sun sets and the colours run to black. I slept well and woke before dawn, then re-stoked the fire to ward off a gentle chill in the air while I did a few hours' work on the laptop. The only interruptions came from visits by an inquisitive young camel that gurgled and stomped around for half an hour or so, and a small flock of galahs that entertained me from a nearby tree.

Sometime after sunup I heard a car approaching and ran out to the road to meet the boss from Ilkurlka. He said he was running late and couldn't talk long, but told me I should make myself known to his brother running the show in his absence and take things from there. He'd be back the following day and we'd speak then.

On arrival at the roadhouse his brother sent me to the camp down the road where I was greeted by the boss's wife. It was a strange meeting. It seemed I'd arrived in the middle of an identification session and from the outset she made me feel like the intruder I had unwittingly made myself, a state not improved when she learned I was a journalist. Spread out before me was a semi-circle of native elders being shown a creature from a bag by a number of DECs staff (I presumed), and under a nearby pergola where several more bagged specimens hung from the framework, stood another group of DECs staff including the Doctor I'd been told was supervising the project. But rather than allowing me to walk ten paces and speak with the Doctor, the boss's wife insisted I wait half an hour till the process was completed before I interrupted him. He was terribly busy standing around waiting to hand out the next bagged specimen.

I'd like to say things improved from there but unfortunately they went the other way. While the DECs crew were keen to do the story it seems the boss I'd spoken to that morning had now decided nothing was to happen till he got back. So I duly made camp and waited for his return. Then when he returned I waited some more.

And when he still hadn't made contact after two days of waiting (a full day after his return) I decided enough was enough. I was camped two hundred metres from his house and he couldn't find the time to make a courtesy call to tell me the story was on, or still being considered, or even piss off we're not interested, which would've been preferable to leaving me sitting there wasting time. I had stories to shoot and a plane to meet in Perth*, so I packed up and went. And a rare good news story about Aborigines, complete with cross-cultural collaboration and wonderful vision of the desert and its wildlife, was left untold because a self-important whitefella had decided I was "a bit Leyland Brothers" for his liking, and he'd rather wait for the BBC, I presume. This country can well do without that sort of proprietary nonsense.

*The scheduled rendezvous with my Big City Girl.

THE OTHER SIDE

I took the Anne Beadell Highway from Ilkurlka to Laverton, and while barely enough to get more than a taste of this great desert drive, Claude and I enjoyed the run. Of course there were a few corrugations and the odd stretch of sand, but the road runs east west parallel to the sandhills and we never came close to needing to engage four-wheel-drive.*

I didn't see another vehicle for two days, and the only signs of life were in the visitor's book at Neale Junction. The latest book – supplied by Connie Sue Beadell, incidentally – made for some interesting reading, and among the lyrical waxings of travellers falling in love with the country were some useful references to points of interest and road conditions. From all reports the Highway east of Emu was in poor condition at the time and I was glad permit restrictions forced me to approach Maralinga from the south and therefore miss that section. I'm not an obsessive four-wheel-driver, and while Claude doesn't mind a bit of rough there's always a price to pay. So I see no good reason to drive on a bad road just to be able to claim I've conquered it. As has been said before, the road always wins, one way or another.

The name Beadell is synonymous with this part of the world thanks to Len Beadell, who built many of the roads hereabouts. As a surveyor with the Australian Army he was commissioned to help establish Woomera and the contentious weapons testing facilities at Emu and Maralinga, as well as open up large tracts of

*Which was just as well, because unbeknown to me I didn't have it.

other inhospitable country in the western deserts. Many outback travellers grant him deity status and there's no doubting his road building feats with his Gunbarrel Construction Company are worthy of high praise. As legend has it he bashed a Land Rover through virgin scrub so thick at times he was changing forty tyres a day (a slight exaggeration?) just to pick a path for his bulldozer to follow, signaling to the driver by reflecting a mirror from atop the highest vantage point which was often the roof of his vehicle. But there are also people who hold him at least partly (albeit unfairly, I suggest) responsible for the Maralinga disaster and rate his efforts with scorn. In his defence, nobody knew what impact the testing was to have back then, and indeed I've heard anecdotal evidence claiming he deeply regretted ever finding the Maralinga site once he realised the gravity of the outcome.

This is Princess Parrot country through here and I kept my eyes open for these pretty little birds but saw none. For the uninitiated the Princess is an eye-catching green parrot with a long tail, a blue crown and the most delightful rose-pink throat you can imagine. It is found throughout most of the central desert country but is rarely seen because of the vastness of its habitat and the inconspicuous nature of the bird (plumage notwithstanding). I did see plenty of camels, though, either in great herds or mobs of twenty or so single bulls waiting for enough condition to rut. In breeding season the dominant bulls will break the herds up into harems for rutting, and as each bull weakens, his place is taken by one of the younger bulls coming into rut. Curiously, as I approached a herd I'd often start a number of camels bucking and pig-rooting as if to throw a rider; perhaps young bulls beginning to feel their oats? A couple of languid dingoes and a dozen kangaroos made up the rest of my nature list, the kangaroos becoming more prevalent as I made the transition from red desert to goldfields grazing country.

Laverton is the first stop on the western side of the desert and looks a town poised to open up if the Great Central Highway continues to gain in popularity. I was told the road already carried fifty thousand vehicles a year, and if plans go well to develop the route from Laverton all the way across to Winton in Queensland that number should increase significantly. In any case there are already good mechanical services on offer in Laverton and it was just as well because the desert took its toll on Claude while I wasn't looking – as if to illustrate my earlier point – breaking a rear shock from its mount and blowing one of the dual tyres. I stayed four days to do some editing and get these matters sorted, then discovered a fuel line problem as well and had to make a run down to Kalgoolie for parts.

I've always liked Kalgoorlie; it's a fun place that seems to have retained a healthy sense of the ridiculous. Walking to town one sunny afternoon wearing my loudest Hawaiian shirt over shorts and thongs I was greeted by a cheeky blackfella with a big grin and an even louder, "Hey cowboy!" We both laughed; I looked about as much like a cowboy as he did a punk rocker.

And Kalgoorlie's the only town I know of where you're likely to see a late model Rolls Royce sporting a bull bar. The owner of the car was filling up at one of the service stations so I asked him how she handled the rough roads.

"Like a dream," he said. "Independent suspension; you can sit on two hundred klicks an hour and not feel a thing."

He was in gold and assured me there were more millionaires driving around Kalgoorlie than you'd find in Perth. I tried to talk him into an interview, but he'd only do so if he could remain anonymous; a bit hard to manage with video. I left him to his dreamy bush-basher and pushed southward, taking the back road to Kambalda and discovering the Teddy Bear Highway* in the process.

The first one I saw was about twenty feet up a eucalyptus tree and so weather beaten I thought it was a burl shaped like a teddy bear rather than the other way around. It wasn't till I got out to take a photo that I could tell for sure. Then down the road aways I saw another, then another, and the pattern emerged. At random intervals between Boulder and the Kambalda nickel mine were teddy bears nailed, tied or otherwise crucified to trees along the roadside. It was an intriguing spectacle, the origins of which I could only guess at. Were they a symbol that you were off to work in a man's world at the mines so you could leave your teddy bear at home? Or did the burly miners at Kambalda just like teddy bears up trees? I considered calling in to the mine site to ask a few questions but the weather was closing in.

By the time I reached Esperance it was dark, wet and wild. Claude was being buffeted around and I was happy to hole up in the first caravan park I found. It blew for two days and nights and on the the third day I rose again from the bed. Okay, so I wasn't in bed the whole time but I couldn't resist the biblical line.

Weather permitting there's not much to dislike about Esperance, but one of my favourite things about the place is the Turkish Bakery

---

*I also discovered a Teddy Bear Tree in Murchison Country later on in the trip, with thirty or more Teddies stuck in and around a small shrub on the side of the road. This time, though, I did get an explanation, and was sorry I did. It was a shrine for a young girl killed in a car accident on that spot.

in Andrew Street. There's no reason I can see why there would be a first class Turkish Bakery in Esperance but there is, and if you visit you should aim for a warm pide fresh from the oven.

Another one is the fact that the Shire charged NASA $400 for littering when Skylab debris landed on the town in 1979. Never mind that one of its residents collected a $10,000 prize for being the first person to deliver a piece of the wreckage to the San Francisco Chronicle. Esperance is proud to be a tidy town and nobody gets away with dropping their rubbish. The bill wasn't paid till 30 years later when an enterprising radio jock got his listeners to chip in and make it good on NASA's behalf.

But all these ramblings are well and good if a man can afford to give up eating. I haven't shot a story in over two weeks and it's time I got amongst it.

YABBIE YEARNING

Some stories take forever to tell. I've been shooting vision of theme trees for three trips now and the story's still not complete. I've videotaped bottle trees, shoe trees, thong trees, piano trees, car trees, skull trees, tyre trees and more from all over the country. Then no sooner do I think I'm ready to cut the story than someone tells me of another theme tree I've missed, like a bra tree for instance, and I know I'll consider it incomplete without that vision. I mean, how could I leave the bra tree out? The story would have no support.

Likewise I started shooting a letterbox story on my first go-round and won't finish it till I can find some good letterbox talent. Just what constitutes good letterbox talent I couldn't rightly say, but I'm hoping the cheque's in the mail. Much of what I do I can't explain beforehand, even to myself. Which is probably why I haven't won a Walkley Award for journalism yet. (Though I'm pretty confident I'll get one for the bra tree story.)

By comparison the yabbie story is a mere babe in yarns. I really only started it a month or so ago when I tried to catch a feed of the buggers at Montecollina Bore on the Strzelecki Track. Got nothing, so I decided to keep the story going till I caught some.

I tried again at Copley with a few of the local lads while I was waiting for the new alternator to be freighted and fitted. They took me out to the local retention dam, but even with their fancy traps and soap for bait – the best bait, they informed me, because yabbies are essentially herbivores and only eat meat so it doesn't putrify their water – we caught nothing. Too much water, they guessed, which is what you want from a retention dam, after all.

So after two failed attempts I finally cracked it at Wave Rock, of all places. I mean, this place is famous for rocks, not yabbies. It's granite country hereabouts and any rock too big to move gets a name. Without even venturing far off the beaten track you can visit Victoria, Burra, Thursday, Glenelg, Sandalwood, Skeleton and Strawberry Rocks among many others, not forgetting my personal favourite Bruce Rock. For reasons I'm not sure I can explain I rather like the idea of a rock named Bruce. It's a strong name, a solid name, like something an unflappable brother should be called, or a draught horse maybe. No? Okay, I told you I might have trouble.

Anyway, normally I wouldn't pick a location so obvious as Wave Rock unless I was shooting a tourism travelogue, but I made an exception on this occasion because I was desperate; two weeks without a story had softened my judgement. But the Rock is as spectacular as rocks get this side of Uluru, and the added extras make this a worthwhile stopover. Not only do they have the granite features, but they've also got a nationally significant lace collection, an enormous toy soldier collection, a small but immaculate fleet of restored pre-war motor cars*, a swimming hole as salty as the Dead Sea, an amphitheatre-in-the-making where you'll soon be able to enjoy 24 hour karaoke with crowd-in-attendance, and no doubt more these imaginative proprietors will come up with in the meantime. As the manager said to me, "You can only rely on nature

---

*The restorer was a grazier who would strip the cars, rebuild the chassis and engine, then use the cut-down form to round up his sheep to expose any rattles needing attention, then repeat the process once the body was refurbished and re-attached. An enterprising marketeer might have named the business Sheep Dog Restorations.

for so much."

So it was while I was shooting a story on that lot that I happened to mention my yabbie dilemma and the boys took up the challenge. No problems, they assured me. They'd set the yabbie traps before they went to bed, and in the morning there'd be yabbies, yabbies everywhere.

But the morning came cold and wet and it didn't seem like nearly such a good idea as it had after a couple of wines the previous night. Undaunted the boys lit a fire in readiness for the harvest, and I was impressed by the show of optimism. Then as we stood on the banks of the dam waiting for the fire to make coals, the moment of truth looming fast, the doubts crept in.

"So you're confident we'll catch yabbies?" I pose the question to my two fearless yabbie hunters.

"Yeah, but let me say I've never done this in winter before," Hunter One responds.

"There's thousands in there," Hunter Two nods. "But they go down in the mud this time of year. So getting them out is another trick altogether."

"But you will swim for them if they don't come out," I insist.

"Yeah, he will," they answer simultaneously, each pointing to the other.

It's a jovial affair and the boys make good talent for the video story. Hunter One is the younger of the two, a jolly, round-faced man who quickly nominates his partner as the yabbie guru to parry any responsibility. Hunter Two has a ruddy complexion and the easy laugh of a man who doesn't take himself too seriously either, and together they make as likely a team of Aussie yabbiers as you'll find west of the Great Divide.

"To tell you the truth we're not too confident about the placement of this one," Hunter One qualifies as we prepare to lift the first of the traps. Evidently he's miscalculated his throw in the dark and only managed to land it about a metre out.

I accuse him of hedging his bets but he needn't have worried. The trap comes up alive with yabbies and he changes his tune immediately, claiming he was never in doubt, that he always knew we'd get yabbies. And yabbies we get as the remaining half dozen traps all come up trumps, until we have the best part of an esky full just itching to jump from one pot to the other one we've prepared earlier over the fire.

They're delicious, clean and juicy like a crayfish only with a sweeter, more delicate flavour.* And standing around the fire on that brisk Hyden morning, bantering with the boys as we eat freshly-caught yabbies straight from the pot, I can't think of anywhere I'd rather be.

"I had this backpacker tell me once that this is Australia," Hunter Two says, pausing to peel and dispatch another yabbie. "You know, sitting out in the back blocks, in the middle of nowhere, catching yabbies, and he's having a beer and he said 'This is Australia. This is what I've come to see.'"

Tourism Australia take note.

---

*I shouldn't have been surprised by either the taste or the availability of the yabbies at Kulin; just over the way at Kukerin is the home of the Cambinata Yabbie, widely considered to be the culinary apogee of this back country crustacean.

TIN H◉RSES

Question: Is it possible for a grown man to look dignified riding a tin horse?

I'm getting the distinct impression they're all a bit unhinged in the Wheat Belt. Maybe it's the sparseness of the fields, all that green and yellow as far as the eye can see. Or maybe it's the salinity of their water, I don't know. But they're different over here. Don't get me wrong: I'm not criticising. I'm a firm believer in celebrating our eccentricities. In fact I wish we'd all give the horses a run out of the paddock more often.

In Kulin they let their horses out. I saw one horse standing beside the road drinking a beer. And another one driving a tractor. And another sitting on the toilet reading Playhorse Magazine. And there were horses riding chariots and horses fishing from dinghies, horses made of wagon wheels, drums and hay bales, and horses with guns and whips and swords. They're all part of the Tin Horse Highway, stretching along twenty otherwise featureless kilometres leading into Kulin in the southwest of WA, designed to draw attention to the town's yearly race carnival.

"Yeah, it's promoting Bush Races," my guide says, "and a bit of fun for people who go along the highway, to see something different."

"Oh, they're different, don't worry about that," I assure him. "City folk driving along will look at them and think 'these cockies have got nothing to do; they're obviously bored or touched or both.'"

"Well in any community you've always got hidden talent," he

justifies. "And when someone starts something, others will follow and it just keeps growing."

And apparently that's exactly how it happened. Back in the mid-1990s someone built a rough prototype to point the way to the races, which started the locals trying to outdo one another with evermore outlandish designs, and before you could say *giddyup* the road was lined with horses and the Tin Horse Highway was born.

"It's just scraps, doesn't matter what you've got in your shed or around the farm – there's fuel tanks, old plough tynes, scrap steel out of the headers, fan belt wheels – people use anything."

"Have you ever built one?"

"No, Monte, I know what I want, but..."

"A horse is what you want isn't it?"

"That is correct, but sometimes you think you know what you want but you can't get started.

"We used to have two horses pulling a boat," he continues, "but someone came along and nicked the boat."

"Maybe the horses took off with it."

"No the horses were still there but the boat's gone mate."

My guide is a large, likable local with a willingness to please, but he's a bit flat to camera so I'm trying to draw some humour from him. This kind of colour story gets done every day and if you don't push the limits a bit you end up with pure beige. Sometimes the pushing works, sometimes it doesn't.

We're having this conversation standing before one of the iron horses called Waterloo Boy. The Boy's a fun, green abomination with a forty-four gallon drum torso, flexible air hose legs and a tubular head with a Larsonesque grin, though many of the other sculptures show considerable wit and flair.

"Like Fillypoosis over there, that was done by a girl, and it follows a tennis player."

The tin horse he's referring to doesn't bear any more than a passing shot resemblance to the tennis player I remember – unless Phillipousis sprouted breasts and started wearing skirts towards the end of his career – but it is clever. Its creator is the woman many people give credit for starting the whole Tin Horse craze off, and is perhaps the one in closest touch with its impact: she's the school bus driver.

"The kids must love this," I make my only sensible contribution to the interview.

"Oh, some of the kids…" my guide starts, closing his eyes and smiling at the memories, "…people stop on the side of the road and they've got small kids, and they get on and ride them -"

"They don't," I interrupt with mock derision, sensing a direction to follow.

"Yes they do."

"Oh, that's *sooo* childish." I've got it now.

"Yeah, but that must stick in their memories for a long time. And they probably talk all the way along and it probably keeps them quiet for the next ten or fifteen mile I suppose."

"I wonder if it'll work on me."

"Well, Monte, you never know," he laughs. "You can try these things."

And that's close enough to an invitation for me. I leap aboard Waterloo Boy like I'm auditioning for a John Wayne western, but the bloody thing lurches back and tosses me.

"Ooh, whoopsie! He nearly bucked you off, Monte." And my guide's enjoying it now, he gets what I'm up to and he's laughing.

And he keeps laughing as I mount the beer can horse, risk a ride on the rickety old wooden log horse and climb up for a dink behind the horse and jockey outside the Jilakin race track. Then comes a wild ride on the upright brute with the Emu Export can and a sword fight with Sir Prancelot. I am magnificent, taming the best Kulin has to offer, one by galloping one. These rides are not for children, they are for mighty Tin Horse warriors like me.

The only challenge I decline is the West Kulin Whoppa, a monster of a beast with legs alone standing three forty-fours high.

I leave Kulin satisfied. It's been a big day.

H IS FOR HARMONY

One of the first off the plane she glazes through the terminal like the Queen of Sheba and doesn't see me waiting for her. Then she stops and smiles at me like the miss was choreographed all along, and I forgive her before I even know I'm annoyed. Her kisses are warm but somehow distant, and when she sees the flowers she beams and kisses me again from even further away. Then she remembers her new Italian boots and extends a leg to show me the black leather CFMs*. I make the appropriate noises of approval and she looks satisfied for an instant, before a fresh thought crosses her mind and her expression changes to one of concern.

"Sorry, darling, but I just *have* to find a cigarette," she says, crinkling her nose at me. "Do you mind?"

She knows I do but insists on going through the charade anyway. I shake my head in gentle disapproval and she's gone, off to bludge a cigarette from one of the desperadoes outside, leaving me with nothing but her bags, her flowers and a trailing waft of perfume and alcohol.

My Big City Girl has arrived.

She wants to go to Monkey Mia and Ningaloo Reef because someone has told her they're "awesome".

"But so are the distances between," I tell her, "and there's no way we can visit both in a week unless you want to spend your whole holiday watching the road pass by."

"That's okay, I'll sleep and you can drive," she says, warning me

*Anagram for a tasteless invitation the wearer of knee-high boots might extend to a lustful admirer.

her last slave was dismissed for insubordination.

In the end we compromise on a round trip to Monkey Mia, and true to her word she slinks up the back to lie down even before we reach the city limits.

"It's been a long flight," she justifies. "The flight attendant told me one drink in the air is worth two on the ground." she says, as she giggles her way backstage. Unfortunately the favourable exchange rate takes its toll and she spends much of the first night doubled over outside Claude trying to get a refund. It's not a good start.

The next day we hug the coastline from Cervantes to Geraldton, as beautiful and windswept a stretch as you'll find anywhere, stopping for fish and chips at one of the pretty little fishing villages on the way because she needs some junk food for the hangover. It seems to do the trick and she perks up some, and that night we camp in the coastal sandhills just short of Kalbarri. We light ourselves a cosy little fire but rain chases us inside, assuring one another tomorrow things will get better.

They built Kalbarri on the mouth of the Murchison River and even on a grey day it'll take your breath away. The gorges are ageless red, the sand is heavenly white and the water is a postcard from the tropics. We decide to take a break from the driving and prop for a day or so, setting up a few kilometres from town on the shore of the inlet. It's a rough road in but Claude handles it well, and it's one of those times I'm grateful for his 4WD capabilities.* We pitch camp on a rocky headland surrounded by water, far from the madding crowd, as cute as you like. We sling the awning up, throw out a fishing line and settle in for a bottle of wine over lunch.

* Even though he had none - put it down to blind faith.

Problem is the rain settles in with us and there's nothing much else to do but keep drinking, and just on dusk my BCG decides she needs cigarettes and she's going to walk into town to get some.

"Don't be crazy; it's raining and it's a lot further than you think."

"I'll catch a cab back."

"You'll never get a cab to come down this road, even if there is a cab service in town."

But she insists, so we get the laptop out and Google Kalbarri taxis. There is a service but they close at 5pm.

"How ridiculous. Even on a Friday night?"

"It's a little country town, sweetheart."

"Then I'll get some delivered with a pizza," she says triumphantly, taking the laptop from me and beginning a new search.

"You won't get them to come down this road any more than you would a taxi."

"You watch me," she says. "It's a little country town, sweetheart. I'll offer them fifty bucks and they'll do it."

I watch her sadly, powerless to help. I used to be a smoker and recognise the demons at work here. I remember the desperate lengths I went to in the process of giving up, including wetting my pouch of tobacco before I threw it in the bin, only to have it spread out and drying in the oven an hour later, so I can sympathise with my BCG's predicament. And here's she's got the tyranny of distance working against her as well, or perhaps more correctly the tyranny of remote country town-ness. She's found a pizzeria in Kalbarri only to learn they don't deliver at all, much less to an unknown campsite location "just a little way down the thingumy."

"How pathetic. Friday night and they don't deliver."

"Who would've thought?"

But she misses the sarcasm because she hears the faint hum of a car in the distance. With the rain falling there's no way of knowing how far away the car is, or in which direction it's travelling, but the deductive powers of the optimist are without equal.

"Hear that? That'll be some young hoons out for a spin. They're coming this way. I'm going to stop them and get a lift into town."

She stands and peers out from under the awning into the wet night, desperately willing the car to approach. Mercifully, whoever they are, they don't come within striking range. I doubt I'd have been able to stop her tempting fate with a carload of strange boys to get cigarettes, and I admit there's a part of me that wouldn't have cared.

Then it dawns on her that it's all *my* fault she doesn't have cigarettes because *I* wanted to camp out here "in the boonies" rather than in town nearer the shops. I know there's nothing I can say in my defence so I grin and bear it. Later she claims she was joking but she's not much short of a three-shrink-trick at the best of times, now she's loaded and so am I there's no hope of reading her. Indeed we've got the whole *Dance of Death** thing happening by this stage, and we waltz the night into a corner to mark awful time till the music stops and the fat lady sings an ageless dirge.

The next morning we each wake to our respective remorse and somehow manage to patch things up enough to carry on to Monkey Mia for the dolphins to work their magic. But something's been broken, like a crack in a fine piece of porcelain that can't be seen but you know it's there. I know I can't carry on like this and still do my work, and I tell her I think we should cool it. She consoles herself in the bar and ends up the same way she did on night one.

*Play by August Strindberg about psychological warfare in a marriage.

We're on a merry-go-round that's not so merry.

The last couple of days of the trip are better, but they still feel like a consolation prize to me. We camp in the scrub and cook fillet steak on the coals. We eat ice creams at dusty roadhouses and laugh at the little things again. The milestones rush past and soon we're saying goodbye in Perth. I imagine it's for the last time, but of course life's never so neat and tidy.

MURCHISON CEMENT

Getting out of Perth was about the only thing on my mind. I needed to get lost to find myself again; lost in the bush, lost in work, lost in something, anything would do. And to add to my tenuous psychological state the weather had turned wintery. Perth's another city that doesn't do cold well. Or maybe it was just my mood, I don't rightly know. But I do know I've only got one woollen jumper and I don't live a nomadic lifestyle to suffer cold weather.

I pointed Claude north and drove. I drove through the cold with windows shut and jaw set, through towns with unfamiliar names like Dalwallinu and Wubin, Perenjori and Mullewa. I drove through the wheat fields until the arable land dried up and the sheep dwindled. I drove till I could drive no more and then I slept and drove some more. I drove till the bitumen ran out and my old friend the dirt began, till I felt the isolation was palpable enough to wrap its arms around and comfort me. I drove till I reached Murchison Country.

The Murchison is the second most significant river in the Gascoyne region behind the Gascoyne itself. Yet unlike the Gascoyne River the Murchison River is salty, and the surrounding country is marginal to say the least, being mostly Mulga wash and Kararra over a hardpan base. Indeed the soil is so hard the locals call it Murchison cement. And it's as good as the real thing. They built the new Murchison Roadhouse out of it.

The Roadhouse is run by a young mother of two boys, who took up the challenge after a failed relationship left her adrift.

"I separated from my husband a bit over two years ago," she tells me, "and this was my whole 'turn the page', yeah."

"Are you pleased?"

"I love it, absolutely love it. I'm so proud of my boys, and what we've accomplished in the last two years has been fantastic."

Her eldest boy is a tall lad of about fifteen, who's more than happy to pick up the tools and have a crack at whatever needs doing. The younger boy seems a contented soul who helps where he can and entertains himself the rest of the time. Neither boy appears the worse off for being away from the trappings of town living.

But it's the mother who's made the choice, and the mother who'll be driving the wagon. She's certainly young enough, still, at thirty-four years of age. And she looks a determined creature, with a strong, lively face and dark brown hair pulled up in a pony tail, exposing a full compliment of gold rings in her ear lobes. When she laughs I see flashes of pink and green studs in her tongue.

"Do you see yourself as courageous?"

"Crazy, yeah," she laughs. "Probably about ninety-nine percent crazy."

"Are you mechanical?"

"I can sort of see myself through. And if not, I call on Stretch, my eldest."

"How do you get supplies?"

"We get delivery one day a week. Every Thursday night the truck comes up, and if it's not on it, you don't have it."

It's two hundred kilometres to the nearest town and there's no fallback option in Murchison, which has the dubious distinction of being the only shire in Australia without a town. The shire CEO highlights the remoteness.

"Our state politician once asked me what happens if you get sick out here and I said 'mate you die. You either die, or you live,'" he shrugs. "You gotta have balls of steel to come out here, you seriously do."

And while I'm not entirely convinced that prerequisite applies to the roadhouse proprietor, she's clearly no shrinking violet. She gets some help from an old local bloke who keeps the grounds tidy in return for a can of drink and a packet of smokes every so often, but apart from that and what the boys pitch in she does the lot; the short order cooking, the driveway sales, the maintenance, the cleaning, the running of the caravan park and accommodation. For all intents and purposes she's happily self-reliant.

The contradiction – and there's always a contradiction – comes when I ask her if there's anything she misses about the city. Her instinctive response is to reject the suggestion. But then she corrects herself.

"Oh, I absolutely miss having my fingernails done. Even [when I worked] on mine sites I always had my artificial nails."

I take one of her hands and look at the poor work-hardened, nail-bitten stubs of her fingers and we both laugh. "I chew 'em. Really badly," she admits, giggling like a teenager. And if she had her druthers, she tells me, she'd gladly pay good money for a weekly manicure. It's a tender highlight to a tough portrait and curiously enough it makes me consider things I hadn't thought before. After all, she's not an unattractive woman...

But I'm saying goodbye to all that, at least for now, so I check my impulses and get back to work. A man in my position can't be accepting comfort from his story subjects, even assuming it was was on offer.

Most of the Roadhouse business comes from a steady flow of

tourists exploring the Wool Wagon Pathway. There were once high hopes for the Murchison as a pastoral region and the Pathway traces the history of the early pioneers in the area from Pindar in the South to Exmouth in the north. But their big bash every year is a polocrosse tournament, believe it or not. I had trouble.

"Polocrosse? Out here?"

"Yeah, we have five polocrosse fields," the proprietor enthuses. "We have a huge polocrosse event every July; the middle weekend of school holidays is polocrosse in the Murchison."

I'd always seen polocrosse as a past-time of the wealthy, but of course I had no right being so incredulous. Polocrosse was a sport invented in Australia as a fun way to exercise horses and help riders improve their skills. The Murchison is mainly cattle country these days, with some sheep and goats, and a good deal of the station work is still done on horseback. It's a logical sport to play and no doubt an eagerly-awaited weekend in the Murchison. The proprietor has every reason to be enthusiastic.

I forget to ask her if she rides but I imagine she'd give it a shot if that's what was called for. In fact I suspect she'd get equally excited about goat dancing, if that's what the community was putting on; she's just that kind of person. She tells me she plans to stay at least five years and says she'll happily retire there, especially if they release land and she can start a hotel.

"I promised myself when I was really little that I was going to have thirteen tattoos, twenty-one piercings and own a pub by the time I was forty. I've got another six years to go."

At a rough count I can only see about ten piercings and no tattoos but I don't go there. Instead I ask her if she's got any advice for women who may be a bit hesitant about striking out on their own.

"Let nothing hold you back. A lot of people use their kids as an excuse; kids don't hold you back. Kids just push you along and drive you harder."

Harder, like Murchison cement.

WILD DOGS

I still remember the pretty purple strychnine crystals the dogger carefully poured into the bandage on the trap. And I'll never forget the story he told me about the dogger who mistook his tobacco tin for his strychnine tin; they found him with the cigarette paper still stuck to his lips, grinning the strychnine grin* from ear to ear.

It was in Murchison country, Western Australia, that I got on the dog trail. During a conversation I had with the Shire CEO a chance comment about the wild dog problem in the area pricked up my ears. It's a serious problem in pastoral areas across most of Australia and by no means exclusive to the Murchison, but I'd been looking for an opportunity to cover the story and here it was. A few questions and a phone call later I was invited out to a property run by a man passionate about dog eradication.

The Murchison was originally opened up for sheep grazing, but cattle have lately become a more economically viable option, with feral goats a reasonable sideline. At the risk of offending a handful of the more conscientious graziers, it's probably more accurate to say the sheep ripped the guts out of it and now only cattle and goats are capable of surviving on land unlikely to ever be redeemed. On the drive out I see very little stock of any kind, unless kangaroos can be classified as stock and then we can consider farmers in these parts to be doing very nicely indeed. But there's no doubting the meanness of the country here, with its mulga scrub and rust red

---

*The death mask worn by victims of strychnine poisoning, characterised by a fixed, bared-teeth grin caused by violent contractions of the facial muscles, also known as *risus sardonicus*.

soil, and it's hard to imagine anything thriving.

The property manager is a wiry bushman with a full salt and pepper beard and battered hat turned down square at the front. He's been an active member of the Dog Control Board in the past, but these days he concentrates on trying to keep his own stock alive. I ask him how big the problem is.

"It's costing a lot of people their livelihoods," he says, "because once an animal has been struck* they can't sell them on the open market. Then there are consequences on price per kilo, and where you may have been getting $1.30 you might only get 50 to 80 cents per kilo."

"Is it right across the board: cattle, sheep, goats?"

"Yeah, it's right across the board," he says. "Goats are prime targets because as soon as the dog sees a goat he thinks, 'great sport' and the goats will move out. To the extent that we were getting eight thousand goats a year, and now we're lucky to get just over two thousand.

"And we've noticed a lot of billies have been wethered. Up to about two percent of the mobs we're getting are wethered goats," he continues. "We've had goats locked up in a yard and we could see where the dogs have actually reached in through the railings and pulled the stones out of the goat."

And as grisly as the prospect is of goats being neutered alive, according to the dogger I spoke with it's common behaviour for wild dogs to attack for pleasure.

"One farmer I know sent four hundred goats off to market," the dogger tells me, "and out of that four hundred, a hundred had been

*Attacked by dogs.

mauled. But you don't know they've been mauled because all the damage is internal, and it's not until the butchers cut the skin off that they see the bruising and teeth marks.

"They attack them to make them make noise. They'll run them up and down boundary fences just to make them make noise, because it's entertainment for them.

"There's a mill around here where they killed thirty-five kangaroos in one night. They actually stockpiled them. I've never seen any other animal that will drag carcasses back and stack them up in a pyramid, but they did."

"The dogs did that?"

"Yeah. I've never heard of it before, and nobody I know has ever heard of it either, and yet that's what they done. And it was evident: we were there the day before, and then I went back the next day and there were thirty-five fresh, dead roos stacked up in a pyramid shape. The dogs had done it; there was no-one else there.

"And I've seen them run them into waterholes, especially deep waterholes, and all the dogs will hang around in a big circle around the waterhole and wait for the roos to drown. Same with emus. Dingoes are actually very, very smart hunting dogs."

I caught up with the dogger doing the weekly rounds of his traps and he agreed to let me tag along. He's another one in the wiry bush mold and he's wearing baggy jeans turned up at the cuffs and a broad-rimmed felt hat that accentuates his angular face. I follow his old Cruiser along a dusty track through the scrub until he stops at a water mill. The mills are the focal points of these paddocks and most of the traps are set around the mill dams. On the far side of this dam is a fallen tree next to a fence, and against the tree we find a partially decomposed dog grinning in the trap.

"Yeah, that's the strychnine grin," he nods. "The carcasses break down pretty quick out here, especially in the summer. The strychnine accelerates it."

He releases the dead dog from the trap and begins preparing another set on the other side of the log, explaining the process as he goes.

"There's several ways a doin' it, but this is the way I like to do it." He stands on the trap to open the jaws, jamming his small adze between the blades "so it doesn't snap on me fingers."

Wearing rubber gloves and using steady, practiced movements he takes a small strip of calico material and wraps it twice around one jaw blade to secure the end. Then he straightens the other end out so he has a platform of material stable enough to pour the strychnine onto.

"So that's the bandage?"

"Yep; that's the bandage for the strychnine," he says, opening a black plastic bottle and spooning a tiny amount of strychnine crystals into the bandage. "Gotta use point five of a gram per trap." Then he wraps the bundle tightly and uses wire twitches to secure it.

"And the dog will chew that off?"

"What happens is the trap will be set in the hole that way," he illustrates the lay of the trap in relation to the log, "and the dog'll come along and put his left foot in the trap and it'll go off."

"Why his left foot?"

"Because that's how I'll set it, so the trap's in a position where he'll stop to sniff, then step off his right foot and get his left foot caught. And of course then he'll want to tear himself out so he'll start biting at the trap and tear the bandage and breathe in the strychnine. And once they breathe it in it just goes through their system really quick."

The trap now set and loaded the dogger scrapes a shallow hollow with his stone axe and nestles the trap into the depression. A sheet of newspaper goes over the plate and jaws, and he begins covering the trap with dirt.

"This is the worst part about setting traps; this is where you catch your fingers.

"I used to have a dog with me, a little puppy, and he got out while I was setting the trap and went to stand on it, and as I grabbed him out of the way the trap went off across me fingers and broke two and ripped the nail clean off that one."

I show him the cursory amount of bush sympathy and move on. "So you'll leave the dead dogs here? They're not a problem for other dogs coming around?"

"They're actually a lure. Cause other dogs will say 'oh there's a dead dog there' and come in to sniff it. And I use a podge bucket." He opens up a twenty litre plastic drum and takes out a four litre plastic pot from inside and removes its lid to show me a dark, evil-smelling mix. "I use dog shit as a lure. And I pee in the bucket as well." Then he spoons a lump of podge and gravy on the log he's built the set against, and walks backwards flicking a trail of podge gravy onto the ground for about twenty metres.

Looking back towards the set it looks all too obvious to fool a smart dog. The trap is buried about half a metre from the podge log, and he's built a corral of sticks on either side of the approach, creating a passage to guide the dog in from the preferred direction. As if he's read my mind he says, "Some people reckon my sets are too obvious. But I've known blokes who use white sticks to guide the dogs in, and even put yellow sand on the plate to show the dogs exactly where to step. But I just do it this way and it seems to work. The dogs come in along this fenceline, they smell the trail and go 'oh yummy' and walk into the trap."

He flicks the spoon once more for good measure and puts the lid back on his podge bucket. The closing of the lid sends a waft my way and I comment on the aroma. "Yeah, that's the worst part of my job; when you go back into town everyone tells you you stink."

Surely not.

Of course many people object to the trapping of dingoes on the grounds of cruelty, and a strong push by animal welfare groups has brought about the mandatory introduction of rubber jaws on traps to mitigate the suffering of the trapped animal. There is also a distinction often made between the dingo and the wild dog, especially by those who would see the dingo protected at all costs. One reason is probably cultural: because the dog problem is so irrefutable and the control methods so absolute, if the iconic Aussie dingo can be somehow excluded from the equation it makes the whole issue so much more palatable. Much like the way the domestic cat is excluded from the feral cat problem, yet commonsense tells us they are inexorably entwined. And there are also valid, genetic reasons to support the distinction between wild dogs and dingoes. Though it should be noted the shy yellow dog that we believe first came to Australia about four thousand years ago is bearing less and less resemblance to the contemporary model with every litter whelped.

"We've done a DNA testing programme throughout Australia," the property manager tells me, "and Western Australia is known to have 60% pure dogs left, in New South Wales and Victoria it's about 4%, and in Queensland it's 30% pure dogs.*

"Which means we're getting less and less pure dog coming in, and the hybrids are very bold."

And getting bolder, it would seem. We know a lot more about the dingo now than we did when we got it so wrong in the Azaria Chamberlain** case only thirty years ago. We now know they do attack and even kill humans under certain circumstances – most notably where sustained contact has reduced their natural fear – and with more tourists wanting more bang for their buck, the station manager is concerned it's only a matter of time before there are further fatalities.

"How big are they getting?" I ask him. "Are they growing any stronger, genetically?"

"Yeah, well, a lot of them are crossing with blue heelers and so forth, to the extent that up at Mardie up the top up here, there was a fifty-seven kilo dog shot."

"Fifty-seven kilos? That's enormous."

---

* According to the survey an animal was deemed pure if it carried 75% dingo DNA. The rest of the list read South Australia 57% and the Northern Territory 84%. There are no dingoes in Tasmania because their arrival to the mainland came after the formation of Bass Strait.

**In 1980, nine-week-old Azaria Chamberlain disappeared from her parent's tent at the Ayres Rock campground, with her parents Lindy and Michael claiming the baby was taken by a dingo. The original coronial inquest findings agreed with the Chamberlains, however the NT Police prosecution were dissatisfied with this result and pushed for a second inquest, at which, with no small support from a sensation-hungry media, the Crown succeeded in having Lindy Chamberlain convicted of murder and sentenced to life imprisonment in 1982. After serving six years of her term, further evidence was brought to light and the NT Court of Criminal Appeals overturned all convictions and Lindy Chamberlain was released. A small amount of compensation was awarded for wrongful imprisonment.

"Yeah, and what worries us is the tourists in some of the tourist setups are actually feeding them. And they're actually going to start attacking people. They think, 'oh nice doggy' but it can actually take you out, take a kid out.

"And it's a big worry. A huge worry."

MARBLE BARRED

When Slim Dusty released *A Pub With No Beer* in 1957 he had no idea he was tapping into a vein in the Australian psyche that would carry the song to greatness. Written by Gordon Parsons unwittingly adapting a poem by Dan Meahan, the comical lament about a pub running out of beer was originally released as a novelty B-side offering. But it took off and soon became not only a country hit, but also a favourite with the country-phobic city radio stations of the time. The song struck a chord with Australians everywhere.

Australians love a pub. We associate our favourite pubs with fun times and friendship. We use them as windows to new horizons when we travel. And a town without a pub feels strangely unfinished. As one bloke said to me, "It's the hub of our universe. It may be very small but it's like our church; we get our employment here, we get all our religious knowledge, we get married… it's our font of information."

So when a town's pub suddenly closes down the repercussions are felt well beyond the shire boundaries. And when it happens to be the hottest town in Australia half the world hears about it.

"Town's only pub closes its doors abruptly," said the West Australian newspaper, "…gasping locals wondering where to quench their thirst."

"Sole pub in Australia's hottest town closes, locals angry," said Australian Associated Press.

"Outback Australians face 400 mile round trip to closest pub," said The Telegraph in one of the most sympathetic articles I read. And that's The Telegraph in the United Kingdom, I might add.

The place is Marble Bar, which gained its hottest town mantle after a succession of scorchers back in the last century. And the pub is the Iron Clad Hotel, still standing much like it was built in 1892, a mighty testament to the longevity of corrugated iron.

But if the old pub has weathered the external elements with dignity, it hasn't always withstood the internal turbulence nearly so well, and it's this story I've come to cover. I arrive to find the owner in the process of doing a re-fit himself.

"They left two months early," he says, referring to his previous tenants. "They just basically gutted the joint. Most of the stuff was theirs, some of the things weren't."

He's a thoughtful young man with dark hair and a face full of stubble. He speaks with a measure of calm belying his years, especially given the circumstances. And although his frustration occasionally surfaces, he's not letting it drown him.

"I think their intention was to leave it so it was shut for as long as possible," he says, alluding to the fact they let the liquor license lapse as well, leaving him to re-apply for a new license from scratch.

"Had you dealt with them before?"

"Yeah, well I was their landlord, so…"

"And it wasn't a good relationship?"

"Mate, they were just recalcitrants. Refused to accept anything."

"That's a good Paul Keating word."

"Yeah, well obviously I didn't know what it meant till he used it," he laughs, resurfacing with a bubble of self-deprecation.

He shows me inside the pub, a space stripped so completely of its fittings and fixtures that it looks naked, our voices echoing off the bare skin walls. There isn't a bar stool or wall hanging or even a light bulb to be seen.

"They took the ice machines, all that sort of stuff," he continues, "all the hot water systems out of the units, took the taps out of the units; they took the taps out of the units and threw them down the tip."

He holds my look to see if I get what he's saying. I do, and it's hard to remain impartial and not think the worst of his tenants. But there's always two sides to every story.

"The thing is," reasons one local, "on the legal side of it the leasee, which they were, owns all the fittings. I won't argue about what counts as fittings and what doesn't, I don't know. But the leasee owns the fittings.

"That's the second time it's happened," he surprises me. "Oh yeah, this is nothing new. The first time it happened, same circumstances, where the owner of the hotel didn't want the leasee to carry on, he made it difficult for him, so he had an auction and sold everything. And it's exactly like the pub is now."

Which is out of action, dry. And while it may have happened before, this owner is faced with the added pressure of trying to re-open in time for race day. It's the biggest event on Marble Bar's social calendar and it's only weeks away. So with time and labour in short supply he's left with no option but to pick up the tools and do as much as he can himself. And with a little help from his friends and his suppliers, and a break from the Liquor Commission, he thinks he just might make it.

A hundred kilometres down the road at the Conglomerate Hotel in Nullargine, though, business is booming. Being the nearest liquor outlet, take-away sales have soared. And some Marble Bar locals have even moved to Nullargine for the duration of the "tragedy", with no intention of moving back before it's sorted.

"What's the point in living in a town with no pub?" one of the recently relocated asks me. "No beer, that's a tragedy. Tucker you can do without, but beer…" he trails off, grinning as he leaves what's obvious to him unsaid.

The publican at Nullargine highlights the suddenness of the assault. Delivery takes time in the bush and unexpected attacks like these can decimate stock levels.

"Well, we still had stuff but nothing anybody in the country wants to drink. Pretty much all the cartons of beer were gone. We might have had ten bottles left on the shelf."

Meanwhile back at the Iron Clad Hotel work continues steadily. Walls are being prepped for a fresh coat of paint – there was never a better time – missing tiles are being replaced, wonky doors attended, all the jobs that never get done when serving customers is more important, or when you don't own the building.

Yet it's easy to be critical of the absent. And not everyone was happy to see them go.

"I always got on all right with the previous publican, you know." It's my reasonable local again. "But see Marble Bar's a small town, and quite a few of the locals got barred from the pub for playing up; that doesn't go down too well."

Any more than the whole business went down with the pub's owner, although it seems he wasn't caught completely off guard.

"I always had my suspicions that they were going to gut the place and do a runner," he admits. "But I thought it was going to be after the Cup."

"Ah, the element of surprise."

"So they got me there," he says, smiling wryly. He's been stung, but he's over the shock. In fact he looks like he might even be enjoying himself now, or at least enjoying the challenge. The atmosphere onsite is pretty cruisey. Things are getting done, though not too quickly. There are plenty of laughs. Previously barred locals drop in to check progress, no doubt pleased the new order will see their bans lifted. A pizza and pool party is proposed – "I guess the pool table was too heavy for them to carry" – and the afternoon runs into night. The hospitality is warm and the beers cold – "the pub's closed for business not for fun" – and the old Iron Clad fills once again with the familiar sounds of people living life.

At some point in the night I sidle up to the publican and ask him if he's planning to get a new tenant in.

"No, I think I might have a go at running it myself for a while."

"Ever run a pub before?"

"No," he grins.

And that's when I know he is enjoying himself.

THE FEVER

Gold. Few words conjure up so much with so little. Four letters, one syllable, yet carrying the weight of unfathomable expectation. *Gold*. Say it and watch heads turn. *Money* doesn't do it. *Wealth* won't bat an eye. But *gold* does it in one short, sharp utterance. *Gold*. Say it loud and watch people reach for their pickaxe and donkey. Okay, so the donkey's dead but you get my drift. Shout the word and mind the stampede. *Gold!* The hopes of everyman in one blind promise.

Australia is currently in the grip of gold fever. It's not so much a rush as a steady surge, driven largely by exorbitant gold prices and travelling baby boomers looking for something to do. Equipped with metal detectors so sensitive they'll detect a pin buried under a metre of soil they're out there in their thousands. Tens of thousands. Finding millions of pins. They find a few ounces of gold, too, but more pins and nails and bottle tops.

"And bullet cases and ring pulls and washers," one such prospector I meet at the Marble Bar Caravan Park tells me. "They're *metal detectors*," he adds, emphasising the words for the slow learners. He's not being a smartarse, merely drawing attention to the obvious to make his point.

"And where do you find gold?" I ask him.

"You find gold where you find gold. And the best place to start looking … is where other people have found gold. These old buggers that have found it, you've got to take your hat off to them, wandering through this country, with what they can carry. And they found 90% of the areas; not all the gold but the areas."

"Do you think there's more to come?"

"They say there's more *in* the ground than what's come out."

"Who says that?"

"Anyone that has hope to find some more," he laughs.

He's typical of the new wave of prospectors. He's a likable, middle-aged man who takes regular prospecting trips with his wife in their 4WD and purpose-built caravan. He may have taken early retirement or be enjoying his long service leave, and he shows me gold they've mined from Queensland and Western Australia. During our conversation he indicates just how popular prospecting is with his demographic.

"Apparently Minelab, who make the machines," he says, "can't keep up with the production."

And these machines don't come cheap, either. The detectors alone cost thousands of dollars each. And then there are the coils – the wands prospectors use to scan the ground – and many prospectors like to have a selection of coils for different conditions.

"At what point do you think you're going to break even on your gear?" I ask him.

"Well, go back to fishing," he cleverly deflects the question, "when do you ever break even when you go fishing?"

So it's not about the money, at least not for these people. Most don't need the money. They're doing it for the adventure, the thrill of the chase, the sense of purpose it gives them. Many even see it as a sport and cite exercise in the open air as the main motivator. These are the hobbyists, the amateur enthusiasts who pick over known fields and rework old mullock heaps in search of surface gold missed the first time around.

Then there are the professionals.

A weather-beaten bushy with a white beard and khaki felt hat introduces himself to me as "a busted-arse prospector". He doesn't believe in picking over old grounds with a metal detector all day – "no, bugger that, they get heavy" – so he uses a bulldozer to expose fresh dirt. He's been earning a living from prospecting in the Marble Bar region for many years, and the way he sees it most amateurs are completely unrealistic about their chances of finding gold.

"I know of people who've bought metal detectors and come up here," he says, "brand new six thousand dollar metal detectors – I know because one bloke unpacked it right here; I showed him how to use it, see – anyway, they think they're going to take two steps out the motor car and trip over a nugget without even using a metal detector. Well all of a sudden this metal detector's back on the market for four grand after two weeks.

"No, with that bulldozer and a creek bed that's got known gold in it," he continues, " I know I'll get some gold with that. You just take a bit off the bottom, six or eight inches at a time, then detect it. Bugger this just walking around with a metal detector all day."

He shows me his bulldozer, a stumpy, rust-red machine with a blade at the front and a ripping tyne at the rear; they look a good match, the crusty old prospector and the well-worn earth mover. And he shows me his windmill collection, not only the first I've ever seen but the first I ever knew existed, windmills not being the most obvious collectible going. And then he pulls some gold samples from his pocket; a large specimen mixed with dirt along with a few smaller nuggets; prospectors always seem to have a sample or two for show and tell *somewhere* about their person.

But why gold, I want to know? Above all other metals in the

soil why did gold end up the most prestigious, the most coveted? We have records of gold jewelry dating back to about 3000 BC, although it's believed it was discovered a thousand years earlier in either Transylvania or Thrace. Then around 1500 BC the Shekel became the standard unit of exchange in the Middle East and gold was used as money for the first time; alloyed, it should be noted, with its poorer stablemate silver. It's likely silver was discovered by humans at about the same time as gold, but while the similarities are undeniable – both are shiny, malleable, precious metals that have been prized as jewelry and currency through the ages – it's never been a serious contender for the top spot. No doubt in part because silver is the more plentiful and usually found alloyed with lead (making the mining of it much less romantic than mining gold), but there's also an indisputable mystique about gold that no other metal on earth enjoys.

"So what is it?" I ask Busted-arse, "about gold."

"It's a living," he replies quickly. "It's only a living to me."

"But some people get well sucked in."

"Oh they do, they hold the gold and say, 'oh, look at the little nuggies' and they get really silly about it. And they talk about finding one gram or two gram pieces," he shakes his head. "I only want the big ones. As far as I'm concerned it's just money."

And to many people it's the only money, especially in times of economic uncertainty. In the past decade the price of gold has more than trebled to around $1,400 an ounce, and rising. In contrast an ounce of silver is a humble $30.

So if mining we must go, then let it be for gold. And if we're thinking gold, why not think big?

On the outskirts of town is a substantial metal frame for

something I figure must be mining related. I learn it's a vacuum ore lifter the owner is hoping to use to resurrect an abandoned mine, by enabling him to suck the ore from much deeper than before.

"At present we're down a hundred-and-ten feet," he explains, "and hopefully we'll sink through to the hundred-and-fifty foot mark, and then a sump under that – because water's a major problem."

"Is that what stopped the previous prospectors here?"

"Yeah, yeah, when they hit the water the ore turned to sulphide and the batteries* couldn't treat it. The sulphide makes the mercury on the plates go hard, and the gold just runs out with the tailings. So the battery manager would've said to the prospector, 'Don't bring any more of that shit in here.'"

"So this whole field," he continues with a sweep of his arm, "they sunk to the water and didn't go any further because they couldn't pump it out."

He's a fit-looking sixty-odd and he carries the no-nonsense bearing of a man on a mission. When I first suggest an interview he baulks on the grounds he doesn't have the time to spare. In the end he gives me fifteen minutes, like a doctor's appointment in the city.

I get a quick heads-up on how the ore lifter works, and he tells me once the water issues are sorted he's confident the mine will be an economically viable concern, yielding twenty-nine grams of gold over three metres. I don't know exactly what he means but I don't dare stop him.

"And there's one section within that," he continues, "that yields nine-hundred-and-fifteen grams over four inches. That's what they

---

*Ore crushing and separating plants used by the prospectors to extract their gold.

call the scab; that's what the old timers used to mine -very high grade – and I'll mine that clean, separate, and every two cubic metres of that will give me probably thirty, thirty-five ounces of gold."

And while I never fully come to grips with the mixed measures – apparently gold is found in both grams and ounces mixed up in either inches or metres of dirt many feet below the surface of claims measured in feet, metres, acres or hectares – I do gather that if all goes according to plan the miner with the vacuum ore lifter will do very well.

"It's all still a gamble though," he tempers.

"Of course, life's a gamble."

"Only trouble is I'm going to run out of time."

"In your life, you mean?"

"Yeah, I'm sixty-eight now."

"Well you'd better get cracking," I get in first. "What are you doing standing here talking to me?"

"That's why I didn't want to," he laughs, and he's back to work before I can pack up the camera.

But my favourite prospector is the Bulgarian I find camped in the dirt beside his ute.

His is about as basic as camps get: he sleeps in a swag under the stars, cooks his meals on an open fire, doesn't even have an esky. For company he has a friendly, fat blue heeler bitch named Molly, and for entertainment he's mixing and matching his prospecting gear. The intention is to make a detector that will not only be effective to five metres down, he tells me, but will also identify the metal it detects. "So I don't have to dig iron all the time." He has parts from several machines scattered over the ground, though nothing more unusual than the scanner from a German model. Ostensibly a square of PVC pipe with two carry straps, it's intended to be 'worn' by the operator like an avant-garde, wire hemmed skirt without the material.

"So what's it called, this machine?"

"A gold machine," he laughs, obviously not about to burden himself with too many details. "And here it tells you whether it's gold or silver," he shows me the screen on the detector. "Lead or silver goes up to 60%, aluminium goes to 80%, and gold it goes up to 100% and this red light comes on.

"The rest is easy, just switch it on," he steps into the square and bends to pick up the two straps, "and you walk. Simple as that," he says, relocating Molly as he swings the PVC square into action.

"And you find gold?"

"I'll make wages, anyhow," he assures me. "At least a couple of thousand a week."

"You'll make that, you reckon?"

"Ah, shit yeah. But you can't find it in the pub," he grins, "you have to work all day. If you stay in the caravan park down there, start ten o'clock – you see them they go for a drive, after half an hour they go back." He's referring to my caravan park talent, the first prospector I interviewed, who tipped me off in the first place about "this crazy guy walking around out there with a poly pipe detector."

"Too hot, too hard, too soft, you think?"

He laughs at this so I push him further. "Do you think we're all getting too soft?"

"Well, Australian people does get soft anyway," he answers. "They like easy job."

I agree with him and suggest we used to be tough but not anymore. He tells me he's been in the country forty-five years and seen the changes, the softening. Even admits to some softening himself, and looks forward to his prospecting trips so he can work off the legacy of his city lifestyle.

"What would you do if you found a really big nugget? Keep prospecting?"

"I like doing this because I'm my own boss, I work in my own time."

"So you'd keep prospecting?"

"Well, you go every year, just like a holiday, you know."

"A holiday, you reckon? A five star holiday." We both survey his camp, with the ten litre water bottle warming up in the mid-morning sun, scruffy swag next to his vehicle, coffee pot standing beside the ashes of the breakfast fire and Molly already scratching around looking for shade, and we laugh. It may not be the Hilton, but I doubt he'd suit five star, this bloke.

THE UNFINISHED SYMPHONY (IN H)

My Big City Girl says it doesn't feel properly finished. Like half a song, she says. Or an unfinished symphony, I guess, but she didn't go that far.

Of course Schubert and Beethoven both had unfinished symphonies, but it was good old Bach again who gave us the best story relating to matters incomplete. It's said that once while taking an afternoon nap, one of his sons was tinkling the ivories and left the piece he was playing hanging on a B chord – read H chord – before walking away. This so assaulted the musical sensibilities of Bach that even in sleep he couldn't bear it, and he roused himself to the keyboard and resolved the piece immediately. (For the unmusical, the B chord is a leading chord, i.e. it takes the music forward and can't provide a satisfactory ending in its own right, because it always sounds, well, unfinished.)

Yet I digress; BCG wants to keep trying. Still believes in us, for reasons I can't really fathom. But Christ knows it's hard enough to get anyone to believe in anything these days so I'm reluctant to turn her away. Maybe she's right and I *am* missing something. And maybe it *is* no easier for her back there than it is for me out here. Maybe.

Where I am, incidentally, is Broome, one of my favourite haunts. I spent the weekend selling books at the Courthouse Markets, and now I've linked up with my cameleer mate from previous visits for a trip to One Arm Point, where his saltwater friends have recently had a victory with Native Title Sea Rights. In 2005 a decision handed down by the Federal Court of Australia granted Native Title to the Bardi & Jawi people for significant areas of land on the Dampier Peninsula, but failed to acknowledge the sea rights in the claim. In 2006 the Kimberley Land Council appealed that finding and in 2010 it was overturned, extending the Native Title to include the traditional island and sea territories described in the initial claim. It isn't the Eddie Mabo case*, but it's still a significant win for the locals, and my friend thinks there might be a story in it for me.

Now it just so happens that while we're discussing our plan of attack in the pub we run into some backpackers about to set off on a Kimberley adventure. They are three fine, French fillies fresh off the plane, looking for some local guidance in unfamiliar terrain. But before you let your mind run away with its worst possible influence, neither we, nor they (as far as I can tell), have any impropriety on our minds. Rather, being new to four-wheel-driving and lacking any experience on dirt roads, they are grateful for the opportunity to tag along with us up to One Arm Point while they get the feel of the road and their hired vehicle. Naturally we're happy to oblige.

So off we set: an unlikely convoy of two, me driving Claude the Inconspicuous and the cameleer driving the natty little hire car, with the girls rotating between us. There's not much to recommend about the Cape Leveque Road, and at the time of writing there's still about 200 kilometres of sand, dirt and corrugations to contend

---

*Landmark Native Title judgement handed down by the High Court of Australia in 1992, overturning the concept of *terra nullius* and thereby giving Aboriginal people entitlement to land and sea rights.

with. Even so I'm surprised the girls seem disinclined to get behind the wheel of their car, apparently content to enjoy the trip as passengers.

One Arm Point is an Aboriginal Community of about 300 people at the northernmost tip of the Dampier Peninsula. It has some spectacular beaches, strong tidal currents that rip between the islands at the mouth of King Sound, and a hatchery and trochus shell aquaculture centre well worth a visit. It also has ambitions of developing its tourist potential through various arts and cultural endeavours, and certainly recognises the expanded possibilities the recent court victory has delivered.

The cameleer's "saltwater fella" mate is a decent soul who would have made good talent for the story, only he's almost completely unintelligible. Nobody can understand a word he speaks, or at least none of us. I've heard people trying to assert that Kriol is not pidgin English but an entirely new language, and while I have my doubts about that, this bloke's the best argument they've got. They should take him on tour.

Instead he graciously takes us on a tour of his country to Sunday Island, one of the newly acquired islands they believe has tourism potential. There's a bit of whitefella history on the island, with a derelict mission and an old fishing camp, and significant blackfella history dating back well before and, of course, during the whitefellas' time. But it's a long dinghy ride through turbulent water to get there, and while I admit our visit was brief, I can't see the potential for a major tourist attraction. As part of a greater Bardi/Jawi experience, perhaps, but not in its own right. (I also thought bottled water would never work, incidentally, so by all means scoff.)

Anyway, we get back to the community and I interview a couple of the locals about the native title decision and tourism and what-have-you, but to be honest my heart's not in it. The story's got no broad appeal, I'm sympathetic but I'm certainly not a left-wing idealist who believes every indigenous murmur is newsworthy, and my best option for talent speaks Swahili. It's time to move on. So we collect the girls, who've sensibly spent the day swimming, and head back down the Peninsula. We camp a night at Middle Lagoon before the cameleer and I push on alone, leaving our lovely young charges in the capable hands of a good-looking ringer from Queensland*.

The next time I see the girls is quite by chance at one of the many gorges along the Gibb River Road, where they inform me the brilliant start to their Kimberley adventure soured with our departure. They stayed on another night at Middle Lagoon, then no sooner had they set off the next day than they rolled their little 4WD and wrote it off. What can I say? Tears fall in my wake.

Which reminds me of where I started this chapter; with a dilemma. And after I drop my cameleer mate off I find myself a quiet waterhole and light a fire. I do a lot of thinking around the fire. It usually doesn't help me find answers, but if I let the flames carry me away I do sometimes forget the question, which is just as good and maybe even better. And occasionally the seed of a song comes to me:

---

*Who I later learned did us proud by catching the girls fresh fish, entertaining them with grand stories of the Australian bush and leaving them unmolested. Or at least so I was told.

Sometimes I wake in the middle of the night and I
*   don't know what to do*
Just me and the stars and that old fire light and
*   what to do about you.*

And here I am again, well on my way to another half a song.

But at some stage that night it occurs to me that if the H chord was really a B chord, and a B chord always leads you somewhere else, it's no bloody wonder I can't find the thing.

THE LAST OF
THE NUTTERS

Back before we all got rich on real estate and set off to see Australia the outback was a relatively empty place. There were any number of regions you could explore in peace, and countless roads you could travel and not see another soul for days at a time. As recently as the early 1990s, for instance, the Gibb River Road was still a serious adventure that discouraged all but the seasoned and the foolhardy. But then everybody discovered the Kimberleys and suddenly it became a must-do road with bragging rights attached. Soon every station, gorge and tin pot stop along the way was packed to the boabs with caravans, campervans and buses carrying the gamut of human cargo from tour groups of spritely octagenarians to freshly-minted backpackers. And although it's unwise to comment on unsealed road conditions in the bush – grading, traffic and rain can all make a liar of you in quick time – I'd hazard a guess Main Roads will maintain this road to a reasonable standard now, at least for the annual dry season rush; the tourist dollar depends on it.

Which, of course, is mostly a good thing. Australians are now appreciating their own country like never before, and our foreign visitors are likewise contributing to the distribution of wealth right across the land. Sure, there's the occasional gripe from tourist operators that these 'free campers' don't spend money in the traditional haunts, preferring to park up in groups outside town rather than use caravan parks, for example – and it's true I've driven past bush camps with up to fifty caravans and campervans settled in for the night nowhere-in-particular. But the simple facts are: there's plenty of them, they all buy fuel and food, and if a tourist attraction interests them enough they will pay to see it (however begrudgingly). Who can blame them for trying to save on accommodation costs where they can, especially when some caravan parks charge the equivalent of city rental prices? In any case I see bush camping as one of the great experiences this country still offers, quite aside from any financial considerations.

My concern with the rapid exploitation of the outback, though, its the toll it's taking on our nutters. And before you take offence at my use of the word *nutter* let me assure you I do so with the utmost warmth and respect. For the nutter is not only my stock-in-trade in this Red in the Centre project but also my natural inclination, my instinctive default position. I like nutters because they are original, because they avoid the *status quo* and go their own way. And yes, maybe also because I empathise with them.

Of course where I would say *nutter* some people use the word *character*, but I reject this word on the grounds of overuse. These days anyone who can spin a yarn is a character, or wears a cowboy hat and a lopsided grin with rolly *in situ*. For me these are stereotypes now as prevalent as the tour operators who trot them out to enrich their clients' bush experience. There is nothing wrong in this, of course, and I certainly don't begrudge these characters the right to earn a living promoting an ideal the public wants to believe still exists. But for me by the time they are presented to a busload of tourists they have already joined the mainstream and lost much of their claim to authenticity. The *bona fide* nutters don't join the mainstream; they peddle their individual brand of eccentricity irrespective of surroundings, which is why they tend to flourish away from the populated areas.

Which brings me to my point. I've said before and still believe a colourful personality will expand to fill the available space. But as mainstream Australia becomes more urbanised and begins to encroach on that space, our rarest birds are being denied room to attain full plumage. And as each adventure road gets opened up to the travelling masses, another nest of originality is flushed, robbed, corrupted or commercialised, and soon I fear the bush will be as homogenised as our cities. And like the Mohicans of the North American frontiers our nutters will be relegated to the annals of folklore, romanticised in absentia as they were never fully appreciated in person.

* * *

I wasn't intending to do the Gibb River Road on this trip, but a chance meeting with a few locals in Derby changes my mind. They tell me about a bloke selling ice cream from a caravan along the way, and he sounds like my kind of nutter so I decide to pay him a visit.

I find him about a hundred kilometres down the road on the banks of the Lennard River. His operation is mostly hidden from the road and his signage is hardly designed to catch the rushing tourist's eye. Indeed the little folding placards promising snacks and ice cream look so out of place standing beside the dusty road that I can easily imagine them being overlooked. But the Ice Cream Man tells me they're more often dismissed than missed.

"I hear them on the radio as they drive past, discussing whether it's a joke or not," he says with a twinkle in his eye. "I don't tell them any different."

He's an engaging soul with a keen sense of humour who would have made excellent talent for a video story. But he declines my offer because he's got a hole in his throat – the legacy of a battle with cancer – and to speak he needs to put his finger over the hole. I try to convince him he sounds fine but self-consiousness is a powerful critic.

He is happy to talk off-camera, though, and tells me he used to manage another store further along the road, but when he took leave to deal with the cancer they replaced him. Unperturbed he towed a caravan to where he is now and set up a new venture, fifty kilometres closer to Derby. His tenure on the land is uncertain, but for now at least he spends the dry season months between May and October selling snacks to travellers curious enough to stop. Then he breaks camp and tows his caravan back to Derby for the wet season, leaving nothing but a metal frame for the floodwaters to wash through.

"When it's over the top of this," he says, pointing to the metal frame annexing the caravan, "It's five metres over the bridge." I look across at the bridge standing twenty metres above the river and try to imagine how much water would be needed to fill the gorge. It makes me feel very small.

"Rachel Ward jumped off that bridge," he says grinning, as if he'd read my timid thoughts.

"When it was in flood?"

"No, when she came through with her husband* and Barry Humphries."

It's shameless name-dropping but why not? You sell snacks out of a caravan on the Gibb River Road and you're visited by three of Australia's entertainment royalty, why wouldn't you gloat? He proudly shows me the photographic evidence and I murmur approval. I sign one of my books for him but he doesn't seem nearly so impressed. It's almost enough to make a man jump from the bridge, but I suspect it would be in vain. I move on, eating my ice cream slowly.

The road is a doddle in comparison to the last time I was here but it's still a great drive. There is nowhere like the Kimberley for sheer grandiosity. It out-Herods Herod. The sky appears bigger and bluer than anywhere else, the ranges richer and redder, for Christ's sake even the air seems heavier, like you're being wrapped in the arms of an invisible big bear. And I love the boab trees with their fat arses and winked-out hairdos; they remind me of someone I went out with once, but naturally I can't remember who it was.

At Imintji I meet an embodiment of the urban squeeze I was referring to earlier. He's a man in his mid-forties who first came to the Kimberley because it offered escape and solitude, but now he finds the mainstream running right by his front door.

*Bryan Brown. And to add a *soupçon* of name-dropping of my own: I don't claim to know Bryan Brown well, but I did meet him a few times back in my old television days and knew him well enough to say g'day. I also happened to live in his neighbourhood for a time, and one day I remember passing him on the street and bailing him up to tell him that I'd just been thinking about him, which was true. He asked why, and I told him because I'd been thinking about confident bastards I have known and he came to mind. He laughed heartily and said that's very funny and walked away. I've always liked the bastard for that.

"When I came here fifteen years ago I was pretty happy to be away from society and the rest of the world," he tells me. "But it's caught up with me now."

He runs a small mechanical workshop on land he leases by agreement with the Imintji Community elders, servicing the passing tourist traffic with minor mechanical works and tyre repairs. He's a gentle soul who speaks openly about his feelings for the Kimberley in a way that also hints at the close connection he enjoys with the local people.

"I like the spirit of the place, you know what I mean? I feel the earth spirit. Like when I'm out walking, or hunting, or riding my motorbike around, or even just driving up to my property up the road, you know, like during the wet season, I'm just grinning from ear to ear."

And he shows me photos of his property with the rivers in flood and the grass so green it looks like it can't possibly be real, and of corroborees he was privileged enough to witness, and of billowing black storm clouds building up over red escarpments, and always it is the land in full wet season splendour. And he talks of finding the right woman one day to share it all with him, this country he loves so passionately; but only the right woman, because there is no suggestion of him leaving the Kimberley, at least not for now, not for anyone.

"Do you think it's changing?" I ask him.

"Oh, absolutely. It was an adventure road when I first rocked up. Now it's just a drive. Yeah, there are rough sections, and if you venture off the road it does get rougher of course, but the actual Gibb River Road pretty much is a breeze these days."

"Do you think this is a good thing or a bad thing?"

"I think it's a good thing," he says after some deliberation. "I'd rather see the Kimberley focus on tourism than pastoralism, you know. I mean, every time you open up a newspaper or a travel book or watch a travel show there's always something about the Kimberley.

"But I'm here because I want to live here, you know? I have four months of the year when I make a really good living, two months either side of that when I *can* make a living, and four months *enjoying* the place."

And *that* would be the four months when the rivers are swollen and the road is closed and he has the place to himself again.

Footnote: A funny thing happened while I was at Imintji. I accepted an invitation from the mechanic to stay overnight, and we had a few beers and a barbeque. Midway through proceedings a bright, pulsing light appeared in the southern sky, heading north. It travelled quickly overhead at a level I guessed to be around five hundred feet, and made not a sound. In less than two minutes it had sped across the night sky and vanished, leaving us all wondering what it was. If you look at a map you'll see there is nothing much to the south of Imintji and and nothing at all the to the north, so what a silent, pulsing, bright light was doing travelling at great speed out there was anyone's guess. I showed the video footage I shot – one of the advantages of having camera gear always at the ready – to my UFOlogist mate in Darwin and naturally he confirmed our suspicions that we'd witnessed a visit from his alien friends, and maybe he's right. But if not that, then what?

CAT DOG

The scientist gets me to open the jar because she can't budge the lid. As soon as I break the seal the stink belts us both, a sickly-sweet putrification of rotting guts and formalin. I return the jar and she grimaces as she empties the contents onto an enamel plate.

If you didn't know what you were looking at I'm not sure what you'd think. I know the jar contains the remains of a feral cat's stomach so I'm prepared to see partly decomposed wildlife. Even so I'm not ready for the magnitude of the carnage. Before us is a pile of dismembered bodies that you'd barely hold in cupped hands; the haul of only one cat over one night's hunting.

The scientist is wearing pale blue rubber gloves that look slightly incongruous sifting through the grisly mess doing a body count. "That looks like a Pale Field Rat," she says, inspecting a section of animal in her fingers before placing it with the others on the rim of the plate. "Here's another back end. So we've got one, two, three, four, five six individual animals so far. This looks like a Delicate Mouse so that's seven." She gets up to nine marsupials and one small goanna before she stops counting.

"And this is from one cat?"

"One cat," she says. "In one night."

"Was this a particularly big cat?"

"Floyd *was* a big cat."

So they called him Floyd. They had time to name him because he took so long to catch. And they know it's only a night's worth of kills by the degree of decomposition. And the sobering thing is, this is happening every night, everywhere around the country.

"The Invasive Animals Co-operative Research Centre estimates that there are between twelve and ninteteen million feral cats in Australia," the scientist elaborates. "So let's start with that lower estimate: twelve. We know cats consume between five and fifteen native animals a day, so again taking the lower estimate that's sixty million native animals killed every day by cats. And I don't even want to imagine what that amounts to in a year.

"Australia's got the worst mammal extinction rate in the world," she continues. "We've lost twenty-four species of mammal in the last two centuries. And most of those losses were due to the impacts of feral cats and foxes. At the moment we have no broad scale method for controlling cats. Foxes and wild dogs we can control to some degree by baiting and trapping. You can't do that with cats; they don't take baits, they take live prey. And they're not easily trapped. So we had to come up with a more proactive approach."

So what they've come up with is Sally. Sally is a Springer Spaniel being trained as a cat dog at the Mornington Wildlife Sanctuary in the Kimberley, one of the Australian Wildlife Conservancy's twenty-odd properties throughout Australia. What's expected of Sally isn't that she'll be trained to single-handedly control the feral cat infestation in the north, but that she and other cat dogs may help the land managers detect and catch cats for further research, e.g. to fit with radio trackers to help determine density and behaviour patterns, etc.

Now to me there's something about training a dog to chase cats that sounds a little superfluous. So when I meet up with Sally and her trainer out for an afternoon walk at Mornington, I ask him if it isn't already inherent in a dog's nature to hunt cats.

"Well, it's natural for a dog to chase things that move fast, in general," he tells me in a dancing Spanish accent, "or at least for the so-called hunting breeds. Then you have to be a bit more specific with the dog, and give him the training that he needs in order for him to recognise the targeted species, which in this case would be a cat."

"So how do you make them target specific?"

"Well the most important thing is for the dog to bond with the handler. Once you've done that you can start teaching her. But without bonding, the teaching is almost impossible."

"So are the walks part of the bonding?"

"Yes they are. At present we normally do about two hours in the morning and two hours in the afternoon. Then, when she becomes a bit more confident, I'll probably cut down on the bonding training and then jump into other more complex exercises."

"Such as?"

"Such as exposing her to cats. And such as hunting, and riding quads, and camping out and these sort of things. It's a matter of fitness, mental and physical."

I've met them on a sandy track winding through some classic Kimberley savannah. There's a pair of boab trees growing like Siamese twins on one side of the track and an anthill taller than a man on the other. Knee-high grasses cover the rolling terrain and most of the vertical vegetation is made up of stunted bloodwoods, Pindan wattles, and the ubiquitous stringybark eucalyptus trees. The sky is a beautiful blue and the raucous din of corellas bedding down for the night provides the soundtrack.

Meanwhile, Sally has flopped down on the red sand and lays spreadeagled on her belly, panting. She is brown on white and has a sweet nature, wagging her tail as I kneel beside her and scratch her ears as I speak with her trainer.

"Are there better breeds for this sort of work than others?" I ask him.

"Well, yes, it depends on your targeted species. But for a job like this probably a smooth-haired fox terrier has certain advantages. Sally will eventually get used to it and learn to handle the heat. But in this environment I'd much rather have a dog with shorter hair to tell you the truth."

We resume walking and Sally bounds away, covering five times as much ground as we do by constantly crossing the track and zig-zagging and springing through and over the grass, chasing ghosts and generally having a splendid time. Long hair or not it must be the dream job for a dog. But the trainer tells me such jobs aren't all that scarce, and cat dogs are commonly-used wildlife management tools worldwide, particularly in the eradication of cat populations on offshore islands.

"Have you always been a dog trainer?"

"No, no, I don't consider myself a professional dog trainer. I'm a person interested in dogs, with certain affinities for them, and I have an interest in wildlife management, but I'm not a professional dog trainer, no.

"Probably the most important part of the training for me, is the personality of the dog, that interest in things. And if a dog doesn't want to chase a cat, he's never going to chase it no matter how hard you try. Or if he's scared of cats, he's gonna quit after the first contact. And that happens."

"So you get a long way down the training road and then...?"

"And then they have an encounter, the cat wins, and they don't want to do it anymore."

"Has Sally been in contact with cats yet?"

"Yes, at least twice."

"And she's not afraid?"

"No, she's very enthusiastic about it, she's very happy with chasing cats, and putting them up trees, and chewing them up afterwards," he laughs, as Sally sails over another tussock of grass, brown ears flapping.

But the reality of the feral cat problem in this country isn't nearly so joyous, and the scientist is doubtful the message is getting through. She's not anti-cat, but believes there's a lack of awareness in the public domain.

"I don't think people understand what feral cats are doing to our native fauna," she tells me. "And it's probably because they're so elusive and hard to see. I mean people understand the impact of foxes much better, I think, because the fox has been vilified."

"Whereas a pussy cat is a pussy cat."

"Yeah. Look, I love cats. But there's a place for things, and a cat that's home in suburbia, being well controlled and well managed, is not the same as a feral cat out here, that's eating up to fifteen native animals a day."

"Can we win this battle?"

"Well, we have to win this battle or we're going to lose species. I guess it comes down to a choice that people have to make. How much do you value our natural heritage? There'll always be some people who don't care. But in a lot of cases I think it's because people simply don't have the information. And if they knew the impact that feral moggies had I think they probably would care.

"And of course the trouble with a lot of these native animals is they're nocturnal, they're cryptic, people don't see them, they often don't even know they're there. So if you're losing something you didn't even know was there, that's not going to have an impact. But I think people that are familiar with dunnarts and planigales and quolls and hare wallabies and so on – anyone that knows about those animals doesn't want to lose them."

Do we?

THE TORSO AT LARGE

We are camped on the edge of Kakadu on our way to East Arnhem Land and The Torso is asleep in his swag, currently snoring like a chain saw. Soon he will grunt and splutter and change pitch to something more akin to the whine of an electric planer, or perhaps he will imitate the rumble of a distant tram for a spell. He's really very talented at this. When he first suggested he bring his swag along I was disapproving on the grounds of space-wasting, but now I'm tremendously grateful. These noises he's making are not for sharing.

His swag has always been a bone of contention between us. When he was in the process of buying it he rang me for a recommendation. I told him to look for a basic canvass model. "Keep away from anything fancy," I advised. "If the salesman mentions windows, awnings or fly screens tell him you're after a swag not a tent." Naturally he took no notice and purchased the deluxe Stargazer model – a truly ridiculous piece of camping gear which takes a good half hour to erect and necessitates he carry separate bedding anyway – but at least he's out of earshot.

Before we leave Darwin he wants to buy a portable toilet seat so he can ablute in comfort. Says he's concerned about fouling his legs in the act if he squats, especially if he gets the squits. I assure him I've been squitting squatting all my life and only ever made a mess of my legs once when I was chased out of the scrub by a King Brown snake. This doesn't put him at ease any and it's only the combination of my ridiculing and the salesman's sneering that makes him drop the idea. He's a city boy and the thought of two weeks in the bush without creature comforts terrifies him. When we do the shopping he buys twelve rolls of toilet paper, presumably so he can swaddle his legs in tissue.

But I suspect the real reason he wants to buy the camper commode is because he's a rather portly size these days and he's afraid he may not get back up once he squats down. He asks me to help him curb his binge eating but I joke that I don't really want him losing weight because I'm hoping to sell him to one of the communities in Arnhem Land – by the kilogram. He laughs but later I realise how sensitive he is about it.

He travels with a suitcase large enough to conceal a family of four, filled with French wine and Cuban cigars. To see him admiring his newly-erected swag holding a glass of Cote Rotie in one hand and a Montechristo No. 2 to his satisfied lips is to witness the essence of contradiction. He's the veteran of one previous five day trip into the outback with a friend he claims was too spoilt, "but this," he says with an expansive wave of his cigar around our dry camp in the savannah scrub, "this is living." He's clearly an old hand now.

We eat early as is my wont and by nightfall I'm ready to crash. The Torso hasn't been to bed before midnight since he was eight years old. He's initially bemused by the prospect but accepts it philosophically. "Well I guess there's not much else to do out here," he says, wistfully looking around for a television he may have overlooked in the bush somewhere. Yet in the morning he wakes fresh and clear for perhaps the first time in his adult life and assures me he's seen the light; from here on in he will always be "early to bed, early to rise, makes a man healthy, wealthy and wise." I tell him to be careful making hasty promises and please don't light that cigar inside Claude.

Another of his less than endearing traits is what he calls "doing the hubba bubba", where he fashions every burp he makes into a string of, well, "hubba bubbas". It's an unpleasant sound heard even once, but since he's got gastro-intestinal issues it's on high rotation.

"One day you'll blow yourself up doing that."

"Want me to teach you how to do it?"

"No, thanks. I'm okay for gross party tricks."

"Hubbubbubbubbubbabbaa," he lets rip another one to prove he's still got what it takes.

Being a big man he also feels the heat, and although it's dry season mild he's suffering badly.

"Man it's hot," he says.

"I told you it'd be warm."

"Anywhere you can swim around here?"

"Plenty of places if you don't mind swimming with crocodiles."

"Surely there's somewhere. What about you watch out for me and I'll be quick."

"No way, brother. Too much temptation for me. "

But he misses the aside and keeps on about it until we reach the East Alligator River. There the crocodiles are lined up five deep at the crossing, catching mullet in the swirling wash. They only do this at certain times of the year when the mullet are trying to jump the ford, but it's a sobering sight and he never mentions swimming again.

Then there are the flies and midges. I tell him we all suffer and show him my own bites, but The Torso is taking it personally.

"Try to imagine them as your friends," I advise. But he's having none of it.

"Look at these bastards," he demands, furiously swatting mid-air with one hand and reaching for his extra-strength insect repellent with the other. "Why can't they just leave me alone?"

"They're only bush flies. Go inside Claude and they'll drop off."

"Why's that?"

"Because they don't like shade."

"Amazing," he says, truly impressed for a moment before he thinks it through. "But it's too hot inside the bus."

The next day some permit issues force us to turn around and drive down to Katherine. *En route* we find a crocodile-free spring for him to take a dip. Watching him loll about in the clear water it occurs to me that this is the first time in several days he looks relaxed. He asks me to take a picture and then goes crook at me for framing the shot too wide and showing his guts. I tell him to get over himself, it was just lucky he had a wide-angle lens on or I wouldn't have fit him in at all.

At another dry camp that night we eat and drink well again, and spot satellites and shooting stars in the busy sky. The fire is a comfort of coals and a gentle breeze starts up to keep the midges out of play. We could ask no more and I suggest as much to The Torso.

"Yeah, but I wish that breeze was a bit cooler."

"Want some external air conditioning?"

"Really?"

"Sure," I say, getting up to go inside Claude.

"Man, why you been holding out on me?" I hear him say from outside. "Crank that baby up."

But when I come back out and toss him an A4 folder to fan himself with he doesn't appreciate the joke.

While I sort out the permit the next day I send him out to Katherine Gorge to see the sights and he returns quieter than usual.

"Good fun?"

"Yeah, it was okay."

"Find yourself a backpacker to play with?"

"Nah, they were all old."

"Since when did that ever stop you?" His last girlfriend was about twenty years his senior and "Grandma" was often mentioned in jest, but he's not rising to the bait. In the end I give up cajoling him in favour of polite conversation and go to bed shortly after dinner. In the morning he informs me he hasn't booked his flight from Nhulunbuy yet and they've doubled in price since he last looked. I start helping him look for a cheaper flight but nothing satisfies him. I don't pick it up immediately but he's searching for an out clause.

"The other thing that worries me is we're not getting on so well," he finally admits.

"How so?"

"Well, it's hard, and it's not going to get any easier, is it?"

"What did you expect?"

"I didn't expect you to be so caustic!" came a reply that surprises me by its force.

"Caustic? Give me some examples."

And he recounts a crack I made about him wasting his time reading self-help books – "they're clearly not working, mate" – and some other slight I made about something I didn't catch because I was trying to figure out what was really eating him. The outburst didn't make sense; our relationship had always been adversarial and the jibes never worried him in the past.

Then finally I get it. His image of Arnhem Land as an exotic, tropical wonderland hasn't been realised and he doesn't fancy the prospect of another week of reality before we reach Nhulunbuy. Especially not with someone who won't cut him any slack. And in hindsight I guess I could've been more understanding and less of a smartarse, but at the time I couldn't be bothered.

"What do you think?" he asks me, and I imagine I could have resurrected it from there with a few words of encouragement and a joke or two, but I was in work mode and didn't have the energy to mollycoddle a soft city boy.

"I think if you're going to whinge all the time you might as well take your ball and go home," I say, stone cold. It's not a side of myself I like but I was pissed off at him for trying to blame it all on me, for not being man enough to accept his part in Hitler's downfall.

And as I'm driving him to the Transit Centre I think how true it is that you don't really know someone till you travel with them.

The next time I reach for my torch I realise the bastard's pinched it. He insisted on having it in his swag with him so he could … what? I don't know, spotlight drop bears I suppose. And now I presume it's wrapped up in his swag in Sydney waiting for his next big adventure in the great Australian bush.

EN TERRE ABORIGENE

The chapter title is French for *On Aboriginal Land*. It's also the title of a book written by a Frenchman who runs a tourism enterprise in Arnhem Land. I haven't read the book because it's in French, but he tells me it's slightly controversial. That doesn't surprise me; I've known the man thirty years and never known him to be afraid of controversy.

Neither does it surprise me that he would set up a tourist venture on Aboriginal land. He's always loved a challenge. When I knew him, indeed worked for him briefly, he was in hospitality in Darwin, and his sparring partners were the various Liquor, Health and Building Departments inclined to interfere – as he saw it – with the running of his licensed premises. These days it's mainly the Aboriginal Land Councils and to a lesser degree the Business and Tourism Departments he needs to manage, but he's lost none of his fight.

When I arrive his camp is unattended, but I recognise his stamp immediately – the neat rows of cabins, the understated style, the attention to detail. It smacks so much of the man I knew all those years ago I can almost imagine I'm reporting for work, only this is remote Arnhem Land, and I'm in a safari camp not a restaurant or nightclub. The thought crosses my mind that we never really change through it all; races maybe, but not horses.

There are about a dozen buildings including a couple of amenities blocks and a sizable dining room, and most are of the same basic structure: red rock walls to about a metre, fly screen sides and pitched poly roof to allow flow-through ventilation. The overall effect reminds me of safari camps I've seen in Africa, except the red wash on the rock work is a standout, and comes – I'm told later – courtesy of a termites' nest and water slurry painted on after construction.

The camp is built on a gentle rise above a spring-fed creek I can hear bubbling away as I walk down the slope. The water is flowing clear and the stream is lined with pandanus, their other-worldly foliage catching the eye amongst the more conventional eucalypts, acacias and bloodwoods standing around. It's true of the Top End that it's mostly harsh country relieved only by the occasional waterway, and to find the waterway first look for the line of pandanus.

I park Claude next to the spring and go for a wander, but don't have to wait long before my old friend arrives.

"Bonjour Monte," he says jumping from his rig with open arms. "You are well, no?" His accent is still as thick as his hair, which at least has had the decency to fade. Otherwise he looks the same man, the same horse. The years have treated him kindly.

We talk easily and exchange three decades of news headlines in an hour – there would be time for detail later – and I learn he moved from hospitality into tourism thanks to the generosity of the traditional owners of this country, who gifted him the land to develop the hunting safari camp. He's been living here now for twenty-one years and has forged strong bonds with the local people, particularly those from the nearby Weemol community. He targets only the French-speaking market, and while the buffalo hunters provide the cream it's clear he considers the Aboriginal experience to be the major drawcard.

"What we offer here at Bodeidei camp is a bridge," he says, gesturing with his hands throughout, "between people coming to see a place in Australia where you have no access, and Aborigines people living as today on the land. And all my marketing to the travel agency very, very strict: 'Aborigines people is not for sale. Is not painting, is not music, is not dance'. We not stuck on the 'tourist culture traditional' rubbish," he stresses, mixing the words around and parenthesizing the point with his fingers in the air. "Exactly what's happening is what you see. You like, welcome. You no like, go to see the people dancing in Cairns, go to see the show in Alice Springs, but no coming here."

"What do you think your European clients take away with them?"

"I think people realise, after, that they come to the true Australia, because there's nobody here except Aborigines people. When people going to Sydney, Melbourne, Cairns or anywhere people love it. But it's San Francisco, New York, Paris and London. Here, most people come with family and kids. And I think this land is so open, so beautiful, and still the Aborigines people living on this land is true people.

"So people leaving with one very good sentiment," he continues, "to understand Aborigines people is not just some people with no idea, completely lost – traditional way, of course everything is gone, but knowledge still for the land is existing, knowledge for the bush, to go hunting or fishing – and the objective for the camp is to make people realise that Aborigines people is not the Aborigines people they going to see on the street, or on the newspaper – rape the kids, drunk like zombie, no good with this, no good with that – but here is true Aborigines people."

Commendable ideals, but nothing we haven't heard before. So how does a Frenchman in Arnhem Land manage what seems to be eluding mainstream Australia? As it happens a couple of French families are booked in for the next few days so I tag along to see.

The first thing once the guests are settled is to visit the local community and see who's up for a day out. My friend says he never pushes the point, but he does pay the locals for their attendance on the tours. On this day a traditional owner (T/O) and two of her children come along. She is a strong-looking woman with a ready laugh and no front teeth, and the kids are a girl and a boy of about ten and seven respectively. They all clamber into the open Troop Carrier and we return to Bodeidei to collect the guests.

We take lunch at a billabong some three hours' drive from camp. *En route* there are several pretty creek crossings and plenty of donkeys, buffaloes, brumbies and birds to keep the tourists interested, but my friend concedes the distance between features wouldn't impress an Australian traveller accustomed to sensory overload. Even the billabong, though charming enough, is no Kakadu wetland.

But the tourists seem to be enjoying every moment. Each time we stop along the way my friend shares his understanding of this Aboriginal way or that, and his audience is rapt. At a small waterhole he discusses, I think, clan names and skin names, tricky subjects in any language. At a wash-away he talks about ceremonies and body painting, identifying some of the ochres they use and encouraging his guests to get stuck in. They do, with some amusing results. The lunchtime discourse is about country and the billabong dreamtime stories I suspect, though I can't be certain. In fact to be honest I haven't a clue what he's actually telling them, and can only assume it's *bona fide* because the T/O is never far away, ready to clarify any point of confusion. It looks to me just like any other legitimate tour being conducted by any other experienced tour guide. Except it's in remote Arnhem Land and it's in French. And it's so politically incorrect it's poetry.

"To know the Aborigines people," he justifies, "isn't to come here as anthropologist or linguist, coming here for one specific job and close your eyes for all the rest. You need to come in with your heart, with your human side. And thinking, 'okay I like the people' and try to do something, or 'I no like the people, okay I take my suitcase and I move.'"

After lunch we push on into some rockier country towards, I'm told, our T/O's own country. We stop for afternoon tea at a creek in a shady stand of melaleuca and pandanus, and I notice our T/O off to one side stripping one of the paperbark trees. I wander over to help, imagining I'm getting involved in some culturally significant ritual to do with her land. I ask what she wants the bark for.

"To sleep on," she laughs.

Of course.

Perhaps sensing the crestfallen whitefella was expecting something more *traditional* she continues, "Or sometimes for [wrapping] my roasting meat, bush meat, like fish, emu, turkey, kangaroo..."

"What about a canoe?"

"Yeah, and I can make canoe, too," she laughs again, "make a boat for the little girl."

"How did you learn to do that?"

"I always see all the old people, ladies and old men, but sometimes my dad tell me."

She's what they call an easy drink: easy to talk to, easy to be with. She's even easy to learn from in spite of me not being the best of students. What I do learn though is that she's a *Dalabon* speaker (one of a dwindling number, I discover later) and she's of the *Yirritja* moiety (as opposed to *Duhwa*; everything in Arnhem Land is either one or the other). Embarrassingly I don't remember her skin name, which is very important in Aboriginal culture, but here's how she explains the skin names of her family.

"In Aboriginal way, me I find," she says, meaning *have*, "a daughter and son is *wamutjan* and *wamut*. My brother, him find a girl and boy, him *gotjok* and *gotjan*. My kids him *Dhuwa* and my brother kids is *Yirritja*."

Suffice to say this is all complex stuff for a newcomer and when I put my head in my hands in mock resignation she laughs heartily. I dare say serious students of the clan system could figure out the T/O's skin name from the above information, but all I can tell you for sure is the *Dalabon* word for spider is *mut-ta*, because we found one on the bark 'bed'.

Yet as I said she's easy to talk with and forgives my ignorant whitefella ways – mentioning the dead by name and doubtless other social gaffes I committed during the conversation – and clarifies the gifting of the land to my friend.

"My dad when he was alive, and my mother, they are the one's that gave him the land, with the Land Council, they come with the old people and we had a meeting at Bodeidei, when my father my mother my uncle was alive, and they gave him the land."

She goes on to say how my friend is good to the community, bringing meat and royalties from any buffalo kill, buying groceries for her in Katherine, giving the women and children somewhere to escape to when the men start drinking. At the mention of the old community problem I remember a story my friend shared with me earlier.

"The old *balang* one day told me," he said, using the skin name to refer to one of the aforementioned T/Os who gave him the

Bodeidei land, "'what kill us, and kill all the kids,'" he quotes the T/O, "'is when naturalisation came in, when the Government told us we are Australian. And the day we been Australian, we move onto the land, people build up house, they give money – we know is bad, but we can't stop the kids to take this money and going to do what all the white people done, going to drink, going to the city, because they been free. And we lost all generations, slowly and slowly, since 1967, since we been naturalised. It was better people keep us as before, because we still get our family very, very close, and we still get our ceremony very, very secret. The day we been Australian we been completely opened; meaning, you are Australian, like us, now you're going to living like us.'"

Again this irreconcilable view is not a new one. But it is worth remembering.

The rest of the afternoon is spent fishing and swimming in the downstream waterholes, but there is one incident worthy of recall. After a time we split into two groups and the tourists to go up the hill to another swimming hole, while we start making our way back to camp. The terrain is rough and our passage slow enough for the T/O's young girl to jump out and start lighting fires behind us, and my friend goes crook on her. It's one of those quandaries kids present you with where you have to make a clear choice. Is she right to be lighting fires in that country, given mosaic back-burning is a natural part of the locals' land management regime and she's probably seen it done many times before? Or is it irresponsible, as my friend asserts, because she is potentially jeopardising the lives of the other carload of people who could easily get isolated by the blaze? To me it's clear cut – the kid isn't old enough to be making those judgement calls – but there are others in our vehicle who disagree, who feel that regardless of her age, because she is Aboriginal she knows what she's doing. God help us.

It's been a big day and I can see why our European friends find it so rewarding. Coming from their gentrified surrounds the Australian bush must appear wild and exotic to say the least, and the local representation on the tours would give the experience authenticity. The commentary seems informed and sympathetic, although I can't imagine my friend glosses over the gloomy realities of Aboriginal life in contemporary Australia. Is he a little biased in his views? Undoubtedly; he's indebted to these people for the means to operate his business and it would be suspect if he wasn't. But is this such a bad thing? I think not. And surely the alternative isn't pretty.

And maybe it doesn't hurt to hear an outsider's opinion every now and then.

"I think the perception of Aborigines people in this country is not right because the story is too long," he explains. "The past story for Australia is past. We can't go over. I a foreigner for this country, I have nothing in touch with the land, and I think this help me very, very well to get strong relationship with the people. My approach to the people is very soft, I listen, I try to understand. I never boss the Aborigines people, I never thinking for the people and I never decide for the people, because I want to understand the people. And when I start to understand the people I realise how complex and how beautiful been the system before, and I realise how many things possible you learn from these people."

Note: The English translation of *En Terre Aborigène* was released in 2011.

CARNIVOROUS
BANANAS

There's something about dogs eating bananas that's all wrong. Like cows eating their own placenta after they've calved. It's obscene. As kids we had a scraggle of cats that ate pumpkin peelings, but only because there were about a hundred of them and they were always so hungry they ate anything. These dogs are as well-conditioned as any and have no right being vegetarian. Yet there they are sitting on their haunches begging, if you please, for lumps of banana. Go on, mate, sling us a bit, willya?

Mind you they are good bananas, I have to admit that. The best I've ever tasted, in fact. And I've had them from all over. The sweetest from Carnarvon and Coffs Harbour, grown at similar latitudes on opposite coasts, and from the Top End of the Northern Territory. And of course the North Queensland supermarket banana, compromised a little on taste but doing the job of feeding the country. But these bananas the dogs are eating are on another level again. And the main reason they are superior, I suspect, is because they eat cane toads. The plants do. Not the bananas. Or the dogs. The dogs eat the bananas, the plants eat the cane toads. Got it?

Okay, here's the story. In Yirrkala in north east Arnhem Land is a banana plantation that was set up by the Methodist missionaries in the 1960s.

"In those days people were fairly enthusiastic," the current plantation manager tells me. "There were lots of women worked here and chipped away at weeds all day."

"Yolngu*?"

"Yolngu workers, yeah. And the mission people were often Fijian or Tongan, agriculturalists." He nods almost imperceptibly to emphasise the point; he's not one for grand gestures. "Then the local church kept the farm going after the mission pulled out in the 70s," he continues, "then Yirrkala Dhanbul took over in 2003. And it's currently run by Bunuwal Industrial, which is an Aboriginal company that employs Aboriginal people."

"Is it more difficult to employ Aboriginal people since the Intervention**?"

"Yeah the CDEP*** program isn't as flexible as it used to be, and it's not conducive to people working in places like this. It's mostly unemployment now, I think."

He's too polite to go any further. He's been running the farm for 20 years and seen the indigenous work initiatives come and go. But at the risk of oversimplifying, tinkering with the CDEP scheme by

---

* The indigenous people of north east Arnhem Land.

** The 2007 Federal Government's controversial **National Emergency Response** to the dire state of Aboriginal living conditions in the Northern Territory, which divided public opinion with its radical changes to welfare, land tenure and the permit system among other elements of Aboriginal living in the Territory. It was a bi-partisan agreement and the Intervention was adopted by the incoming Labour Government, but in the recent words of its original architect, ex-Indigenous Affairs Minister Mal Brough, "It has become stagnant and buried in bureacracy. It is no longer working." To which statement we must add the qualifier that we never saw Brough's original vision working either, whether because there wasn't time or it was also flawed is a matter of opinion.

*****Community Development Employment Project** implemented by the Fraser Government in 1977, to address the high indigenous unemployment levels resulting from the Whitlam Government's decision to grant award wages to Aboriginals. Put bluntly, when Aborigines were given equal standing in the workplace they were no longer as attractive to their main employers, namely the pastoralists, so they became unemployed.

both sides of government seems to have achieved little more than put more people on welfare. Indeed, the current model tends to offer almost no incentive to work because it pays about the same as the dole – so why would you? And it's equally discouraging for many employers because the allowable 17.5 hours doesn't give them enough time to get the job done.

So these days the plantation manager runs the 15 acres of bananas without permanent staff. For anything labour-intensive he enlists "a bunch of Yolngu that work quite well" from the Bunuwal Industrial Grounds Maintenance crew. But most of the day-to-day running he manages with his wife, who helps with "pretty much everything", and his teenage daughter, who helps catch the cane toads they feed to the plants. Which brings us back to *Bufo marinus*.

"So why the cane toads?" I ask the manager.

"Panama Disease," he answers simply. "Tropical race number 4."

In short, Panama disease is the scourge of the banana industry worldwide. It is a fungus that enters the plant through the roots and cuts off supply. There are four different races affecting every commercial variety known to the industry. Tropical race 4 attacks the dominant Cavendish variety and to date has been confined to the Northern Territory (and some Asian countries), but there's a very real threat it will spread to Western Australia and Queensland. It cannot be eradicated and once a plantation has been affected it's only a matter of time before production stops. The manager points out the wilting leaves of an affected plant, then fells it with one blow of his machete and shows me the tell-tale brown spots in the cut of the stem.

"So you use the cane toads as fertiliser?"

"Yeah, I'm trying to improve the soil health, and that way increase the bananas' resistance to getting the pathogens."

"How did you come up with the idea of cane toads?"

"They're readily available. And they're also a problem in that they eat worms, and if you can increase the worm population in your soil they spread the nutrients around and produce their own fertiliser. But if you've got cane toads eating them all night it decreases the fertility of the soil."

So he and his daughter trap toads in wire mesh cages baited with fluorescent lights (to attract the insects, which in turn attract the toads) and make mulch from the carcasses. He takes me to see his mulching plant. At first glance it's clearly a work of art. He's got an old farm ute chocked up on its own back wheels, with the rear axle driving a series of gears and shafts rigged up to a cement mixing bowl. At some stage the bowl has been painted pink, but now there's a fetching brown splash staining one side, perfectly replicated in two halves like a kiddies' symmetrical art painting. How it got there I didn't ask, but when he starts the ute and gets the bowl turning it looks like part of a set from a 1970s psychedelic theatre production. I think my observation was, "She's out there, baby."

"Yeah, we mix them in there with some cardboard boxes and a bit of anything we can find, leaves or banana waste, fish carcasses, and it comes out in about ten days and it's quite a nice compost."

I like the way he refers to it like you might refer to a cake fresh from the oven, even though it stinks like a dead cow.

"I've been away and it hasn't turned over for a few days," he apologises. "But if I turn it over three times a day it keeps it aerobic and it doesn't smell, there's no flies."

"And do you see a difference?"

"Yeah, I've experimented with blocks of paw paws, and the ones that have had the cane toads have fruited earlier, and they've been a lot healthier plants."

As well as bananas he also tends a small orchard of red paw paws and limes, about the most exquisite tropical fruit combination I can imagine and again the best I've ever sampled. Though he admits diversifying won't prolong his stay. The needs of the local market are easily met with the plantings he already has, and freight makes the export market cost-ineffective.

Likewise he knows the cane toad mulch is too labour-intensive to be a serious defence against Panama Disease on any commercial scale, even if improving the soil health does make a difference.

"It'd probably be cheaper to set up somewhere else, but there's nowhere else around here to go, so we've got to look after this bit of country as best we can."

"So really once the bananas go, your job here is done."

"Yeah," he nods. "Unless they come up with a new variety of banana that's resistant to it that we can plant out."

Which would be a great shame. Not only because we'd lose a delicious strain of banana, but what would those dogs eat? While we've been hooning around the property in the manager's golf buggy the dogs have been tagging along. There's three of them. The largest is a brown Doberman called Rocky. The next down is a tail-less blue dog called Clyde. And Midge is a little brown and white fox terrier cross. And they all eat bananas. Rocky even picks his own, then brings it to be peeled and tossed in sections into the three waiting mouths. As the manager says, "They know a good banana when they see one."

AT THE FEET OF
THE MASTER

I'm getting blown away by a didgeridoo. And I don't mean figuratively. I'm being cleansed, apparently. The operator has agreed to let me interview him but first I have to be blown out. A bit like a spiritual pull through, I guess. He obviously knows something about the media. So I'm sitting opposite holding one end of the instrument while he blows into the other. And I assure you it's no insignificant thing to be blasted by a didgeridoo at point blank range. He starts with a series of short, sharp blats then eases to a steadier drone before tapering off with a controlled piping. I can feel the sounds resonate through me. I've got the bell-end cradled in my hands, directing the flow into my body, my neck, my face. I feel like an executioner who's turned the gun on himself. My eyes are closed, I can smell his breath, sweet and strange, feel its warmth on my cheeks. It's an intimate experience. All up it lasts about three minutes and when he stops I'm not sure it's been enough to purify my soul but it's certainly woken me up.

I'm in East Arnhem Land with the man many believe to be the guru of the didgeridoo, or *yirdaki* as it is called here. Indeed with us are two of his students; one has travelled from Newcastle, Australia, and the other from Sicily, Italy, just to be with the master. I know absolutely nothing about the *yirdaki* and even I had heard of this man and his extraordinary craftsmanship. I knew people paid big money for an audience with him, to sit at his feet to learn his gifts and make their own *yirdaki* under his guidance.

Yet the man is not what you might imagine. Though humility is best depicted in deed it seems to me his manner is entirely unaffected by his reputation. When I arrive at his modest house he comes to the door and greets me, then invites me to sit with him outside with that minimalist flick of the wrist so typical of Yolngu people. I take the chair he offers and sit quietly while he and his sister discuss what to do with me.

Humble or not they are discussing money, how much to charge me to do the story. I don't usually pay for stories because I barely make enough to cover costs as it is, but I agree to pay him a little. It's my small concession to cheque book journalism, to mainstream. His sister quotes a figure and I almost choke, which at least stops me running the old *only want to borrow it, not buy it* chestnut. They confer again but I save us all further embarrassment by saying what I can pay. He nods, she says okay, and the deal is done.

The meeting has come about purely by chance. Indigenous stories can be difficult to arrange because they often need approval from several sources – i.e. traditional owners and Land Councils and sundry other gatekeepers – who aren't always on the same page. (Or even reading the same *book*, sometimes.) But it was the Newcastle student who found me sitting outside the Northern Land Council office in Nhulunbuy and offered me an introduction to his master. I still followed protocol and informed the NLC, but it was the student's recommendation that provided my entree.

The Novocastrian is a slightly-built man of about forty years, with a healthy pink flush and a flop of greying brown hair. He tells me this is his second meeting with his *yirdaki* master and when I ask him what the attraction is he answers with unselfconscious reverence.

"As far as I'm concerned he's the man," he says. "This is the man I'm able to sit with nice and quietly and be me, know who I am and my connection to the land. And *he* shares that connection through *yirdaki* and through his heart.

"In short I always wanted to play a musical instrument but didn't know what I wanted to play," he continues. "Through circumstance I was introduced the didgeridoo. So from then I started to play, but I taught myself. Then I heard about this man up in Arnhem Land who you go and spend seven or ten days with and learn what I thought was the didgeridoo. But it wasn't.

"I used to play didgeridoo but now I play *yirdaki*," he qualifies. "So I play differently, in a different way. And it wasn't till I sat down with this man and his family, and he played that *yirdaki* of my heart, and it changed my whole way of seeing things and being. I still play the instrument, but it comes from a different place inside of my heart. Now I play *yirdaki*. And I have a better understanding of what it is, its truth."

"Do you think it's a road to spiritual enlightenment?" I ask, and he pauses and scrunches up his face in deliberation before responding.

"I feel it's a road to my heart. Don't know about spiritual enlightenment, but to my heart."

"Well evaded," I say, and he laughs. He might be getting well out there but he hasn't lost sight of land.

The Sicilian student is likewise fluent in the deft art of grounded spirituality. He's brought his own family out from Italy to visit the master's family and see the land of the *yirdaki*, and he also believes there are connections to be made through the instrument.

"Because I find a cultural association with Sicily, with the traditional instruments of Sicily. Last year we did a festival about traditional wind instruments in Sicily and we invite him and his wife and his sister," he says, with a polite nod to the master. "And then they invite us in Arnhem Land, so we are here."

"So you think there are cultural or musical associations between Sicily and Arnhem Land?"

"It's a long story, but yes there are. It's a long process in Sicily coming back to the roots of the land, and somehow these people are bringing some enlightenment to this process."

"Finding the roots of the music?" I ask.

"The roots of the connection between man and the land."

"Through the *yirdaki*?"

"Through *yirdaki* and through music. In Sicily there is also a traditional wind instrument, like a bagpipe. But it's not the problem of instruments, it's how the connection is still alive in the culture between man and the land."

We're having this lofty discussion sitting on plastic chairs in the back yard of the master's house. At the rear of the house is the workshop where he makes his highly-coveted *yirdaki*; not much more than a belt sander on a stand and a pink wooden bench seat. A pile of wood shavings and half a dozen unfinished instruments are the only other positive signs of industry. Behind us the back yard slopes down to the Arafura Sea, with nothing but a narrow strip of white sand and a few palms and a frangipani tree in-between. The one discordant part of the equation is a siren from the nearby alumina refinery, which sounds long and loud every few minutes. It's an interesting juxtaposition.

The master is a very cool-looking unit indeed. He's wearing a blue and white Hawaiian shirt over blue shorts and has a flowing

THE BEAUTIFUL
Above: *Mitchell River Afternoon, QLD*
Below: *Karumba Lovers, QLD*

THE CAMPS
Above: *Wynbring Well, SA* (story page 38)
Below: *Arnhem Paradise, NT* (story page 134)

THE WRECKS

THE DAMNED

Top left: *Hangin' Out, North QLD*

Top right: *Low Fliers, via Burke & Wills Roadhouse, QLD*

Bottom left: *Fat Dogs, St George, QLD* (story page 4)

Bottom right: *Before the Carnage, Darwin, NT* (footnote page 172)

THE BIZARRE
Above: *Skull Tree, Trans Australia Railway, SA*
Below: *Appliance Tree, via Mt Isa, QLD*

THE CHALLENGING (story page 217)
Above: *Koolatah Crossing, Mitchell River, QLD*
Below: *Claude Dreaming, Mitchell River, QLD*

THE BEARS
Above: *Teddy Bear Highway, via Kalgoorlie, WA* (story page 72)
Below: *Teddy Bear Shrine, Murchison Country, WA* (footnote page 75)

THE SIGNS

white beard rising grey as it meets his hairline. His skin is a rich reddish brown like a strong black coffee with a dollop of cream, and he never removes his sunglasses. He wouldn't look out of place on stage in any happening musical outfit.

His English is halting and a little cryptic at times, but understandable enough to convey the gist when he explains the painted markings on his *yirdaki*.

"That three there," he says, pointing at three rings around the upper end of the instrument, "something like that when you stamp, signature, mean no-one can take it."

"So that's your name, your mark?"

"Yo. One, two, three. From my heart."

"And this story?" I ask, indicating the more elaborately-painted mid-section of the *yirdaki*.

"That story, thunder and lightning, sitting down in the water, different colour. I call it *minke*. Different colour. Sitting down. When the lightning come down and they're sitting down in the water. Different like blink, blink, different," he explains, using his fingers and thumb to indicate a flashing effect. Which I take to mean the story represents the light play from an electrical storm over water, especially when lightning strikes the water. But I'll happily concede a more learned explanation.

He explains how he walks for half an hour in the bush to find the right tree for a "quality *yirdaki*", and then applies glue cladding to the ends to make it both user-friendly and clear-sounding. I deduct from the pile of shavings and a basic knowledge of trees that there's also a degree of carving and hollowing involved to reach a finished product.

The *yirdaki* he's using today, though, isn't one of his own.

It's slightly bulkier than his, with straighter edges and a more pronounced flare. The paintwork is also simpler and more battered and worn.

"This one from America," he tells me. "A present gave me; but hand-made, two pieces."

"That's two pieces of timber cut down the middle and hollowed out and glued back together again," the Novocastrian clarifies.

"You like this sound?" I ask the master about the American model.

"Yeah, because it's light, up," he opens his hand to the sky. "That one deep," he points to his own. "When I young, very… more power…" and he pauses, then gives the Yolngu flick of the wrist and the faintest of smiles to finish the sentence. And I may be wrong but I believe he's trying to express the universal frustration with aging and just can't find the English words. And I wonder how it's said in *Yolngu Matha*, his native tongue.

But in any language the *yirdaki* speaks the same. It's a warm and natural sound rather than a manufactured one, perhaps because it's a very simple instrument. It's basically no more than the breath of man through a hollow log. There's not even a reed to interfere with the flow, save the one made by the user's lips. Indeed by this criteria it's surely as close to the human voice as instruments get. And there *is* no more compelling sound to the human ear than the human voice.

A friend of mine tells a story about the late, great Pavarotti when he was brought out to Australia by the record company my friend was working for at the time. They held the standard industry *meet and greet* affair, inviting all the usual suspects and wannabes, and at a predetermined time Pavarotti sang a few songs. My friend was astonished by the reaction of the crowd.

"I couldn't believe it," he told me. "One minute I was standing in a room full of noisy drunks, then the second Pavarotti started singing, every conversation in the room just stopped dead. And here was this short little guy, no microphone or nothing, just filling up the whole room with his voice."

And don't tell me there were no H chords in the room that day.

So if one *yirdaki* sounds a bit like the human voice, does three sound like a choir? Well, no. It's not quite so literal as that. But they do sound full, and comforting, and *organic*. There are no sharp edges, no stops and starts, none of the silent intervals so important to more sophisticated music; at least not to my ear. Only the rhythmic droning of three differently pitched *voices*, harmonising to a beat tapped out by the master with a small stick on his *yirdaki*, against a backdrop of washing flapping on the line, dogs sleeping in the sand at the feet of their master, and the plaintive wail of the refinery siren.

BLESSED ARE THE GATEKEEPERS

Look out! I've found another rabid gatekeeper. And this one bites.

I wanted to go to the Garma Festival but the gatekeeper said my work didn't fit their image. "The board found it inappropriate", she told me over the phone. So I went to the festival site in person in the hope of finding a compromise but ran smack bang into my new best friend the gatekeeper again. She wasn't pleased to see me. Instead she directed me to get off the land immediately. And no I couldn't discuss it with her superiors; I'd already been told a dozen times I wasn't welcome and if I didn't leave now she'd have my permit revoked. I tactfully corrected that it was only once and she shouldn't exaggerate or her nose would grow so long she may not be able to look down the thing properly anymore, but she blew up and threatened to sool "the board" onto me. "Do you want a rollicking from them?" she warned me in absolute seriousness. I nearly wet my pants: I must have been a very naughty boy to be threatened with such a bad thing. Then she told me to piss off and never come back. It was so much like a Monty Python sketch I thought she was going to pick up a stick and beat me off the premises. I left before she got the same idea.

Garma is the cultural festival hosted by the Yolngu people of east Arnhem Land. Every year a small number of devotees old and new come from all over to camp in the bush outside Nhulunbuy for a five day taste of the local way of life. It wasn't the only reason I was there but it was certainly the reason I'd chosen that time to arrive: I thought there might be a few interesting stories in the mix. Problem is I submitted my application too late and was refused media accreditation. And that's where it would have stopped had the gatekeeper not let slip the "inappropriate" remark. I don't like it when people use that word about my work; it makes me feel like they know something I don't. But most of all it makes me wonder about things like censorship and control and just what constitutes appropriate anyway?

Assessing my work to determine its inappropriateness told me the lateness of the hour wasn't a real problem. So what offended them so much that I was treated like a criminal when I fronted? Was it because my work is occasionally iconoclastic? Or in contrast too mainstream, heaven forbid? (My own industry thinks I'm a fully-liberated nutcase!)

I checked my website for anything offensive but there was nothing obvious to me. The irony in the lyrics to the song *Red in the Centre* could be construed as racist by someone who didn't get my point, I guess, but only if taken out of context. And an old radio interview called "Arnhem Land Hunting" may have crossed the line slightly, but it would take a very sensitive soul to take exception when all parties were so clearly enjoying themselves. In any case I'd argue that sharing a laugh is about the best thing we can do for interracial harmony, and likewise to sell a message in the media. There are still people around who remember things I did on the weather twenty years ago so don't tell me humour doesn't work.

And then it dawned on me: maybe that was it. Maybe I was dealing with someone who remembered me doing the weather "black face" all those years ago.

I know there's a tendency for causists to take things way too seriously. And I've also known such people to be intolerant of those who don't share their views, believing the rest of us unqualified to voice an opinion about the "Aboriginal condition", for instance, and certainly in no position to joke about it. Academics likewise can sometimes indulge in intellectual snobbery and be very funny about humour, particularly in their own fields of expertise.

But surely the people running an event of such significance couldn't be so inflammatory, could they? And even if they did find my work truly abhorrent that's no reason to treat me like something you might scrape off the soles of your shoes. Surely a professional who's driven 600 kilometres of dirt road on spec at his own expense deserves a hearing, at least? Let's not forget Garma is a publicly funded event and I do have a right to ask the question.

The Garma Festival is run by the Yothu Yindi Foundation, and presents an over-riding image of sharing and co-operation, or to borrow a quote from the official website "A garma is a sort of place — of rich resources for many people... all yolngu used to come to this thing garma, coming together, all different groups."

Which makes it all the more ironic that the organisers seem intent on running the festival like their own private party, especially when they accepted $150K of tax payers' money this year to "increase attendance at Garma". How can they justify turning away an experienced journalist who can deliver them to new markets in the face of such a handout?

Of course in some ways this is indicative of a broader, prevailing attitude. The permit system provides a buffer against scrutiny by the Australian public, and the relevant bureaucracies make it very difficult for the media to report from within protected zones. While there's been much talk about lifting the permit requirements for journalists, to the best of my knowledge this hasn't happened yet and access remains problematic.* On this trip, for instance, the Northern Land Council head office issued me with a permit to travel extensively through Arnhem Land sourcing stories, then revoked it *en route* because another Land Council office determined there wasn't enough detail in my proposal. Of course this sort of inconsistency isn't uncommon in any public service department, but it does cast doubts over the suitability of the organisation to manage such a complex and politically volatile portfolio as Aboriginal land tenure.

Meanwhile many communities continue to be controlled by a powerful few operating as a law unto themselves. Never mind the potential for profiteering if the outside world is let in, *it's already happening*, and under the protective cloak of the permit system – the running of contraband, the embezzling of funds, the stand-over tactics. And more importantly women are still being bashed, children are still being abused in every imaginable way, and nobody's game to say a word. Add to this mix a worrying escalation of racial disharmony – I've spoken to female community workers who've been threatened with spears and even shot at in one instance, I've heard of cars being 'borrowed longtime' without authority (at impromptu road closures), and witnessed with dismay a marked increase in the angry anti-white slogans painted loud for all to see. Believe me or not as you see fit but this stuff is still going on; we just don't hear about it because the people who see it happening don't speak out for fear of losing their jobs, or worse.

But getting back to Garma, I'm led to believe this is a brand new

*It's not necessary to obtain a permit to enter Aboriginal land if the visit is at the invitation of a traditional owner.

board this year; out with the old and in with the new, as they say. But have they thrown out the baby with the bath water in their push for fresh blood, and lost the corporate knowledge necessary to run such an event? Or is what I experienced a careless manifestation of the new order? One can only hope it's the former.

On return to Darwin I contacted the *NT News* about my experience and they ran a piece that generated a fair degree of comment from the readers. It seems other people want some answers, too.

And either way it seems to me these people need to declare their hand.

If they want to keep running an exclusive show then fine, they have every right to invite all their mates and keep such tight control on the media output that nothing but the airbrushed version gets out. But don't expect the public to subsidise it.

However, if they want to continue dipping into the public purse they must open the event up and make it more accessible to everyone, including those who prefer not to attend but wouldn't mind seeing what they're paying for out there via a fair media representation.

Because regardless of the politics the Yolngu people deserve much better. They believe they have something special to offer and I'm inclined to agree. Though I'm obviously speculating – since I didn't get in – I believe the Garma Festival is a good forum for both Aboriginal and non-Aboriginal people alike. But it'll never fly unless it's allowed out of its cage. And that'll never happen as long as this elitist mentality prevails on "the board".

Footnote: A journalist from *The Australian* newspaper interviewed me shortly after the *NT News* article ran, and in the course of that phone call told me he'd asked the Chair of the Yothu Yindi Foundation, i.e. "the board", if denying me access to Garma had anything to do with the "black face" weather I did all those years ago. He said her response was inconclusive.

BUSH BELLES

A welcome diversion comes in the form of a day at the Wyndham races. It's a bit out of my way, but I'd promised a mate I'd shoot a promotional video for him, so *en route* from Arnhem Land to Darwin I make the detour. My brief is actually to shoot the whole knees-up weekend, but the highlight for me comes at the races in five bright colours.

It's not easy to capture the intense abandon of a country race crowd. These events are big days out in the bush and even by country standards people travel great distances to attend (see above). So naturally they want some bang for their buck, and almost any behaviour not ending with a ride in a police car or an ambulance is considered acceptable, indeed even tame at some meets. This one, though, is a relatively civilised affair and I shoot the usual selection of beautiful girls, silly boys and excitable punters watching their horses finish first, close and never a chance. I speak to interstate trainers, local jockeys, and space cadets who barely know where they're from. I make friends anew and run into an old one I haven't seen for thirty years. And I shoot everything that moves. It's a full day.

And somewhere in that whirl I meet the girls. They are five good sorts all dressed up in retro frocks they've sewn themselves. Each is wearing a different colour of the same design, and they have parasols, poise and panache. Even in a crowd trying hard to impress they stand out. I fall in love at first sight, if it still qualifies as such divided by five. I ask who had the most trouble following the pattern and the one in paisley green puts her hand up sheepishly.

"It's my first sewing attempt," she laughs. "And that's why my buttons are crooked. But I know what darts, selvage and slip-stitch are now, thank you."

"I sew fifteen metre shade structures by the dozen," adds the woman in red, "but dresses are a whole different ball game."

"Show your petticoat," says Green, at which encouragement Red lifts up her skirt to delight me with a black polka-dotted red tulle petticoat, the like of which I've only ever imagined I saw in black-and-white spaghetti westerns.

Then they all start flashing me! Black demurely undoes her top buttons and invites me to inspect the fine stitching of the neckline. "As you can see it's all, like, hand-stitched at the back," she assures me, though I admit I'm having troubling concentrating on the stitching. "And nice, neat button holes at the front."

"As opposed to these machine-made ones," says Green, undoing her own buttons to point out the flaws I barely notice before she leans over to adjust the top of Purple's dress. "Excuse me Monte, but this is the original style," she says, untucking Purple's neckline from inside itself and lifting the flaps up, "but we wanted to get *the girls* out so..." she tucks the flaps back in to expose more cleavage, and gives Purple's *girls* a friendly pat by way of conclusion.

"We made it sexier," concludes the most bosomly of the bunch, showing me again how they did so by turning the lapels of her own floral outfit inward and revealing more than I have any right to stare at like I'm doing. And with license! And so long as I can maintain my professional demeanour I can keep looking. I'd feel like a wolf in sheep's clothing if I weren't so intimidated.

"Except for [Black]," says Green, snapping me out of it. "You know what she said? 'My mother went to a lot of trouble sewing these buttonholes I'm not getting *the girls* out.' But the rest of us? Out they come."

"The evolution of the dress from the 1950s to 2010," says Purple, "is a bit lower. Still elegant, but lower."

I see. And approve, let me say right here and now lest there be any doubt. But amid the buzz of the race crowd and the continuing banter about buttonholes and getting *the girls* out I get the feeling these girls gone to a lot of trouble to pull this off. To begin with they've travelled around 400 kilometres just to be here. And while they all look delicious to a poor, hungry journalist, for most of them the dresses were a serious challenge.

"What did you learn?"

"Patience is a virtue," says Green. "And when you get home from work and you choose to sew, wait till afterwards before you have your first beer. One beer okay, two beers no, three beers stop."

"I was sewing with my mother," says Black, who seems the most conservative of the quintet. "There was no beer involved."

"Was there a sense of satisfaction walking into this event in your own frocks?"

"Oh absolutely," says Green. "To bother to come to the races you've got to get accommodation, we've all got to get the time off, we've got to get transport, who's car, there's a lot of effort. But as we were walking out, some other lady at the hotel said, 'That's what I used to wear to the races.' And that was enough for me, you know?"

"Would you do it again?"

And all five girls answer "yes" or "definitely" as one.

"Have you got enough attention today?"

And all five girls answer "no" or "not enough" as one.

Sorry Black. I think you're going to have to get those *girls* out after all.

MARKET STRATEGIES

One of the wisest things my father ever told me was, "Nothing stays the same."

The first time I drove into Darwin was barely five years after Cyclone Tracy* had levelled the place and the population was around 70,000. The newly-gazetted Palmerston was little more than an undeveloped sub-division and there was effectively nothing between there and Darwin. At that time there was a point on the Stuart Highway, maybe ten or fifteen kilometres out, where one crested a small rise and the lights of the distant town became visible for the first time. I remember it being an exhilarating moment, coming after a long drive "up the track", and the warm night air heady with tropical scents shaped my olfactory blueprint of Darwin forevermore.

I lived in Darwin for over a decade thereafter and came and went many times, but failed to notice the changes happening under my nose. When I finally left in 1991 to pursue a television career in Sydney it felt as if the Darwin I was leaving behind was the same

---

*On Christmas Eve 1974 a tropical storm that had been largely ignored by Darwinites – because it was Christmas, the system was heading away, and there was a prevailing complacency about cyclone warnings after a number of false alarms – changed tack and savagely belted the town, destroying over 70% of the buildings and killing 71 people. It was a very small, intense system classified as a category 4 cyclone, although the recording instruments were blown away after clocking wind gusts to 217 kph, and there is no shortage of evidence to suggest Tracy was actually a category 5 cyclone with gusts to 300 kph. In any case the town had to be almost completely re-built after the blow and Tracy remains the most devastating cyclone this country has ever seen.

one I first encountered. Yet nostalgia is a potent prompt and each time I visited I tried to find that "first glimpse" spot on the highway, but never did. The city lights had crept out to meet the times. While I wasn't looking the town named after the father of the Theory of Evolution had grown up.

Now, in the thirty years since that first impression, the population of Darwin has almost doubled. The city centre is barely recognisable from the one that opened its arms to me in the 80s, the satellite suburb of Palmerston alone houses 25,000 people, and the once-deserted roadways are now regularly congested with traffic, just like any other grown up city.

But Darwin isn't like any other Australian city. While all places have their points of difference few have so many as Darwin, considering its remoteness from the rest of the country, proximity to Asia, high Aboriginal population, tropical climate, weather and war torn history, crocodile-infested waterways, and the list goes on. And I've no doubt being the capital city of the only substantial Territory in Australia further adds to its individuality. (Yes, the ACT is a Territory, but for all practical purposes it might as well be part of NSW.)

For me, though, what epitomises Darwin's uniqueness is its markets. From the infamous Mindil Beach Sunset Markets, to the more locals-oriented Parap, Nightcliff and Rapid Creek markets, not forgetting those further down the track at Palmerston, Coolalinga and Berry Springs, there's a market experience for all tastes. And if there's nothing to excite the senses quite like a tropical market then there's nowhere quite so sensual as Darwin. I'm not sure whether it's the Asian influence, the steamy, naked humidity, the showy sunsets, or just the fact that most market goers are on holidays (at least in the dry season), but there's a looseness, an air of freedom about these markets that's quintessentially Darwin, and I love it.

And so it's to this libertine hotbed of tropical sensuality that I fly my Big City Girl up to try one more time. What better place to reconstruct a relationship?

Unfortunately it's not one of my better ideas. To begin with I'm at the markets to sell books, so my focus is divided. I need to do this every year to avoid starving. I do have a national distributor, but they're not in it for the love of authors and I'm not in it for the glory. And hand-selling at markets isn't a passive exercise, at least not for me. It's a performance, a full-on game of contact, tag and release where the object is to get as many books out there as possible, whatever it takes. I've tried the laid back approach and almost died of hunger. So now I go for it: I engage, seduce, cajole, reassure, flatter, laugh and jest; in short I sell myself to sell my books. And it works. But therein lies our problem: all the energies I should be putting into her, into us, I'm using up in the sales. Then probably because she's feeling left out she starts getting sensitive about my selling techniques, especially with the women. And she's already suspicious about the French fillies, now BCG's over-reading my flirting for fun and profit as well!

To be sensible for a moment, though, I don't blame her. I'm sure my behaviour looked disrespectful, and it probably was. But likewise when you're totally innocent approaching sainthood as I surely am, it gets a bit tiresome justifying yourself. So I guess I just stopped caring. And if the Perth mess was mostly her doing I have to take responsibility for Darwin. I simply wasn't there for her. Like the mate I took to Arnhem Land I reached the point where I couldn't be bothered anymore, had more important things to do. So I let it all go. I'm sorry girl, I know you tried. But I'm looking for the H chord, and I think you're a Bb.

Footnote: While I was struggling with my own dilemma a parallel tragedy was unfolding back at the B&B I make my home in Darwin. I'd been watching the progress of a couple of curlew chicks being raised in the adjacent paddock, when one morning I rose to find the chicks gone and the adults behaving strangely. To personify I'd have said they looked forlorn, standing well apart and not going into a crouch when I approached. I saw them several times over the next few weeks, running around the house or over by the pool, perhaps looking for their lost babies. But the day I left they were back in their usual haunt at the bottom of the horse paddock as if to signal the end of the mourning period. There'd been a hiccup and now it was time to return to the more pragmatic business of getting on with it. I took it as a clear sign it was time for me to move on as well.

NEVER NEVER LAND

The faster you run from yourself the quicker you tire.

Mataranka positions itself as the Capital of the Never Never on the back of Jeannie Gunn's popular books set on nearby Elsey Station. It's a very Australian term, the never never, and can mean different things. Most often it's used as a romantic reference to the land beyond knowing, beyond reach, or perhaps broadly speaking the great Australian outback before we all went out there and buggered up the myth. Kind of like a geographic H chord. From that meaning it's only a small step to the vernacular use relating to credit, "Put it on the never never." And likewise not a long bow's draw from its psychological manifestation, where someone has not only *found* the never never but found it *to their liking*, and decided to spend more time out there than sanity recommends.

This guy could easily slot into the latter group and be dismissed by polite society, I've no doubt. But I like fringe dwellers, so when I heard about a young bloke living in a humpy in a moonshine fugue I was intrigued. He turned out to be not so young – about my age, which is only young relative to old and vice versa – but such a complex and slippery soul I'm not sure his age was the least bit relevant.

His digs on the outskirts of town are elaborately slapdash. They consist of a shade cloth roof over lengths of black polythene irrigation pipe bent in half-rounds for framework, beneath which he's got all manner of lifestyle effects including a bath, gas cooktop, microwave, refrigerator, freezer and at least one, possibly two caravans. There's also a couple of hefty wire dog cages with corrugated iron lids just off-Broadway, a couple of water tanks, and a tropical garden growing through the lot – which is why I'm not sure about the second caravan; it may have been a pop top trailer converted to permanent use instead. In any case there was definitely a second enclosed space that I didn't enter, because most of the interesting stuff was either outside or in the (other) caravan.

"It's mainly all just re-collected stuff just put together," he tells me. "Because before this I was out bush proper, didn't have no transport most of the time so it was mostly pushbike or leg, and I just hunted like that. Which was the way to go because all the buffs* are already machine-shy."

The man is slightly-built with a beard of salt and pepper stubble and a well-groomed mullet haircut. His broad nose looks like it's been broken at some stage and the lines on his face are deeply etched. He tends roll-your-own cigarettes constantly, smoking them when they're alight and worrying them when they're not, and has a way of cocking his head to the side when he listens that reminds me of a parrot in a cage.

Instinctively I know he'll answer anything I throw at him and I guess I take some liberties I wouldn't take with a more self-assured target. Even so, sometimes I'm not sure when his answers are his truth rather than the actual truth, and I wonder if it really matters anyway.

---

*Asian water buffalo that were introduced to the Top End of the Northern Territory as a meat source in the mid-1800s and soon became a feral pest, spreading right across northern Australia, damaging wetlands and posing a threat to the health of cattle stocks. In the 1980s the Brucellosis and Tuberculosis Eradication Campaign (BTEC) brought numbers back under control, all but destroying the buffalo hunting industry. The machines he referred to were the 4WD bull catching rigs used to muster live buffalo.

"Do you feel as though you're getting further away from civilisation?" I dive straight in.

"I've already been out there," he says. "Nothing but a knife, blanket, dogs. Already been out there like that."

"What about in your thoughts? Are you getting further out there, do you think?"

"That's a hard one, because in one way yes, and in other way no. It actually brings out the best in civilisation."

"How?"

"Because it draws a focus on the best parts."

"What does, living alone?"

"No, living rough. Not having anything, just going from river to river, knife, dogs and that's it."

And not for the last time he artfully sidesteps the question, though whether purposefully or he genuinely misses my point it's hard to tell.

I count at least three dogs living with him, good-looking Ridgeback-style dogs that aren't as heavy-set as Ridgeys in the body, though perhaps a little squarer-jawed. A white one skulks around the corner and out of sight and I ask him what breed they are.

"My own, really. I started off breeding Ridgebacks and Mastiffs, then I started breeding my own breed, Outbacks. It's just refinement now, but I don't have the space here to build up the numbers."

As we talk he gives me the cook's tour, pointing out various curios as we go; an Aboriginal grinding stone he rescued from the bulldozer's blade, a home-made donkey he uses to heat his water, his banana and chili plants, some home brewing equipment...

"Is this where you brew your beer?"

"No, in the caravan. Want me to show you?" He leads the way.

For reasons I couldn't tell you I'm not surprised the caravan isn't being used for sleeping.

It doesn't look much like a brewery – with plastic 20 litre drums instead of stainless steel vats for brewing and re-commissioned 2 litre soft drink bottles instead of glass longnecks for bottling – but it certainly smells like one. He makes a double-brewed black stout using honey for the second ferment and he points out a couple of the drums popping with batches ready to bottle, and behind us the shelves are laden with full bottles. He obviously takes it seriously and I ask him what alcohol content of his brew is.

"Oh mate, don't drink and drive on one bottle, and try not to walk too far on three." Black Gold he calls it. Sounds more like black death to me.

"Do you find you spend a fair bit of time wasted?"

"No, not really," he replies, scratching his head. "You just enjoy a good drink. But there's things to do. So I'll get up, and I might start at four o'clock in the morning and get all the house gear things done, and then go off and do gardening or whatever else is needed to do, maybe go and do a quick hunt to fill up the freezer for the dogs."

"What are you knocking over: wallabies?"

"Only on permit down here, 'cause there's a national park alongside."

"What about road kill?"

"Road kill I do," he smiles. "No shame in that. Fresh meat."

"And you're a reader?" I say, noticing the shelves full of books in the brewery.

"Oh yeah, I've got a passion for books, I tell you. I read and read. I had a library out in the scrub and that was the hardest thing to carry around. But reading and all that kind of stimulation does help your mind. All the old people I've ever talked to say if you don't use it you lose it."

"You don't think you're negating one with the other?" I grin and point from the bookshelf to the beer shelf.

"Life has gotta have the joy and the sadness," he chuckles. "It's gotta have balance."

Fair enough. We move on, past the reindeer horns and the Australian flag, past the rabbit traps and the cray pots, past the pumpkins and marrows just ripening...

"So have you still got family you keep in touch with?"

"Yeah, yeah I do."

"And what do they think of you living like this?"

"Well early days..." he starts, then rethinks his answer and doesn't answer at all, "well even back then, because of the economics of the country if you didn't get off your arse and go out and find a job you didn't get one. And once you get the bug for travel and the bush gets you, then there's no coming back."

...past his paw paw plants growing in soil he tells me he's regenerating, past a hurling stick he found on the side of the road...

"Do you know what this is?" I ask him, picking it up.

"Yeah it's from that Irish game. There were two of them, but I use one to stir the home brew."

"I'm sure the Irish would approve."

...past the kitchen sink and the old meat grinder re-commissioned as a toothbrush holder, past his "Mexican siesta" bed that he uses when it gets too hot to do anything else...

"So how do you live? Are you on unemployment benefits?"

"No, disability." I throw him a quizzical look and he continues cryptically, "Other things can happen in your life and you change direction."

"What things? Was there something quite pivotal?"

He pauses to think. If there was something it's no longer available for immediate recall. Too painful, too long ago, I don't know, but he looks genuinely lost for an answer, with not even the alcoholic's friend confabulation to help him out. And when he does respond he skirts the issue and talks in platitudes, concluding by telling me it's been a long journey getting back on his feet.

"So do you think you are getting back on your feet?"

"Yeah, in a way. But there's good and bad times. Now I'm looking at the other things I can do."

"Such as?"

"Art."

"Show me some of your work."

"Well there's only one I got left now." He leads on, past the casserole simmering in the electric frying pan..."all the others got destroyed" ...past the radio tuned to the classical FM station... "there's only one left and that's just a practice to get used to the oils again" ...to a couple of large, busy paintings* that aren't the worst I've ever seen in that style, but don't exactly jump out at me and say, "Take me home!"

"Do you get into the home brew and work or do you work sober?"

"Sometimes I have a nip," he admits. "But I won't be full-on doing a Blue Poles if that's what you mean."

"Have you done oils before?"

"Yeah, I used to. Whenever I could. But travelling around so much, most of the stuff you carry disintegrates, if you're really

---

*He rings me a few months later to clarify that only one of the paintings was his; the other was done by his girlfriend at the time.

hitting the tracks."

"So all the trappings of civilisation…"

"Fall off you," he finishes my sentence.

"So if you had your druthers and you could do anything you wanted to do, be anything you wanted to be, what would you do, what would you be?"

"I don't know," he says, and his eyes cloud over again as he takes a long toke on his rolly, "that gets back to your earlier question about the pivotal things, events in life that can take you off your path on different tangents… I know I probably would have gone to uni. I was going to uni anyway."

"To study what?"

"Art was one, history, and I'd have to say science."

Which all sounds about right according to what he's shown me. But I'm still none the wiser about his pivotal moment, if there was one. Did something catastrophic happen to this man to turn him away from the civilisation he was obviously a part of at one stage, or am I looking for an H chord here? Do we reach the never never by design, step by stealthy step, or come upon it suddenly, by accident? And again, does it really matter?

"Women?" I ask him suddenly.

"Oh, mate, you'd be surprised where you find women," he grins. "Or where women find you."

"Is that right?"

"I don't miss out in that regard. And interesting women, from all over the world, you get to meet different types."

"Do they find you fascinating?"

"Some find you fascinating. But if you don't find other people fascinating then we may as well all be clones." He's grinning broadly now, enjoying himself.

When I leave we exchange gifts – a book for a bottle of devilish black brew – and I still don't know whether I've been talking to an enigmatic original or a fascinating loser.

BITING SNAKES AND KIDNEY STONES

In the early 1970s a young man drives from Brisbane to Darwin in his VW Beetle. On the roof of his car is a box containing two pet snakes. The way is long and hot and when he reaches Mataranka he takes the snakes out to cool off in the springs. He finds a quiet pool and they all swim together as natural as can be for a man and two snakes *to* swim together. Then returning to his car some tourists spot the man draped in snakes and a crowd gathers. The commotion attracts the attention of the owner, who comes to investigate, and the young man's new career as a tourist guide begins.

"We used to do croc spotting tours at night," he tells me, explaining how they'd cut the motor and drift in quietly, fixing the torch beam on the red eyes until they were close enough to hoist the crocs from the water and into the boat, so the tourists could get their picture taken holding a crocodile. "Only Freshies, and nothing too big. But the tourists thought it was great. Then we'd let the crocs go and drop that load off and take another load out to do the same over again.

"And in the daytime we did four-wheel-drive tours. But it got so busy we had to put another bloke on. And I had to train him.

"Now this bloke wasn't too keen on snakes. And I told him when a snake crosses your path it's good for business to grab it and show the tourists. But they move quick, so don't try and pick it up properly or it'll get away, just grab it and let the thing bite you and you'll find it doesn't hurt.

"'Oh, I don't know about that,' he said mimicking a timid voice, 'I don't know about that.'

"I said look, they've only got small teeth, they won't hurt you. And you can't be handling snakes if you're afraid of them. Just let it bite you and you'll overcome your fear.

"Anyway, we come across this snake and I say here's your big chance, get out and grab that thing.

"So I stir the thing up a bit and he leaps on and grabs the snake and it hits him twice on the arm, a little bit of blood trickling out," he continues, indicating on the inside of his own forearm where the snake struck. "And he's holding the snake up, proud as anything you know, and I says, now did that hurt? And he says, 'no, I didn't feel a thing.' I says, 'there you go' I says, just like I told you it wouldn't. But there's only one problem: that snake's deadly poisonous!

"Well, his face dropped, he threw the snake up the air, and I never ever saw that snake come down. It's probably still up there somewhere. Of course the snake wasn't poisonous at all."

My jolly storyteller looks a lot like the American actor Robert De Niro with an Australian beer belly. Another similarity is he doesn't *tell* stories so much as perform them, gesticulating grandly with every toss and turn of the plot and doing voices in character. I'd even venture it's lucky he's got a few teeth missing in front or he'd have fans asking for autographs. There's no doubt he's an amusing package, and it's easy to see why he's never been short of a tour guide gig at Mataranka Hot Springs, ever since he first swam his snakes here thirty-odd years ago.

"It was the third most popular place in the Territory at the time," he tells me. "Behind Ayres Rock and Katherine Gorge. In those days you had to bribe the bus driver to call in. Even at the Gorge.

But we had five buses a night in here then."

"So Kakadu and Litchfield weren't even on the radar yet?"

"No. And I used to do fishing tours out in the billabongs and guarantee you'd catch a barramundi or your money back. And when I was doing those tours there was only three of us doing it; two in Darwin, and me.

"Back then the industry was run by the Northern Territory Reserve Board from Alice Springs, and they had all these old fogies, and no money. And they didn't encourage tourism because they would've had to spend money, on roads and facilities and everything, so they actually made a lot of the places harder to get to. If you went out to the [Katherine] Gorge, for example, that was the roughest corrugated road you ever met, and there was no camping ground or anything, you know?"

"Could you see the potential of Mataranka then?"

"Well, Mataranka was a little place then, about a third the size it is now. And I thought it's gonna be like that forever, you know. But of course it never is. And now it's an international stop-over, as far as tour buses are concerned. Before it was just all Australians. You never heard a foreign language or saw a backpacker for years, you know.

"There was no house here, there was only half the buildings, that toilet block was here. There were no powered sites, no electricity, we had generators out the back, and just a dirt road coming in."

There's a mural painted on the side of the toilet block in question, of a river scene with an athletic young man catching a barramundi. I take a wild guess and ask my guide if it's him.

"Yeah, I was in my early twenties, yeah."

"You haven't changed a bit, brother."

"No, I haven't, have I," he laughs, like I imagine De Niro does when the cameras are off and he's taking the mickey out of himself.

And we walk through the grounds that *have* changed a bit, past the homestead and the hotel complex, along the bitumen road to the expansive camping area, and down to a pathway leading to the thermal pools. Once in the forest the Livistona palms tower above us, filtering the sunlight before it reaches the heavily-matted floor. An occasional fan palm or paperbark grows here and there and pandanus palms hug the banks of the river, but much of the forest floor is bare apart from the Livistona trunks and countless layers of dropped fronds. Sitting stock-still an Agile Wallaby watches us intently, waiting till we are almost upon it before hopping away. A hen Shining Flycatcher settles for a moment beside the path, her black and white and tan plumage striking an exotic note in the dull green light. And from somewhere overhead the grating screech of a corella reminds us we are still in Australia.

This is also a well-known habitat for the Little Red Flying Fox but I don't see any on this day. Apparently they've been brought under control by the novel method of installing sprinklers in their roosting trees and dousing them with water whenever they try to roost. It may sound a bit over-the-top, but for the management of the park the bats were becoming a serious nuisance, cited as a reason many tourists were bypassing the Springs. So they sprung them with spring water. Although why a creature that handles wet season drenchings would find a squirt of water so offensive is hard to fathom.

"The Leyland Brothers* turned up here one day," my guide

---

* Popular Australian adventure documentary makers who had their own television shows in the 70s and 80s, introducing Australian viewers to the outback.

continues. "They used to be my heroes, the Leyland brothers. Used to watch them on TV, going through mud and dirt tracks and over the roughest terrain... anyway, they turned up here just after the wet and wanted me to show them around all the *We of the Never Never*** country. So I said, yeah no problem, we'll go out, but we might get bogged; there's a lot of water laying around.

"He said, 'Oh, can we take your vehicle?'

"I says, what's wrong with your vehicle?

"And he says, 'I don't want to get it dirty.'"

And I gather by the pansy voice he uses for the Leyland Brother's response they slipped from their pedestal that day.

We walk on, coming to a crystal clear spring that my guide tells me is the start of the thermal system. He explains the water bubbles up from limestone aquifers that extend for hundreds of kilometres. Indeed it originates from a number of subterranean sources including the Georgina Basin, which just happens to be the largest Neoproterozoic-Palaeozoic basin of the North Australian Craton, for those of you clamouring to know that little pub trivia gem. But more useful to know, I suspect, is the fact that the water comes out of the ground at about 30 degrees Celsius, which is what makes Mataranka such a popular spot. As you would expect the water is limestone rich – indeed Mataranka boasts the only limestone quarry in the Northern Territory – but it also contains high levels of diffused salts and many people swear by its curative properties. My guide, however, is not convinced.

"It's terrible water," he says, "it just clogs everything up in the pipes, fittings, all the trouble under the sun, yeah."

*I assume this was just after the release of the movie of that name, based on the novel by Jeannie Gunn.

"But as far as aches and pains go, doesn't it cure certain things?"

"Yeah, it'll give you bloody kidney stones or whatever, that's about all," he laughs. "It's full of calcium. People do come up here every year and go for a swim in the pool thinking the minerals will do them good, but it hasn't got much minerals in it."

So maybe the bats know something about that water, after all.

BRICK BY
HANDMADE BRICK

Sometimes, in spite of myself, it still all works out for the best. It's this way at Roper Bar.

I arrive at the store without the faintest idea what I might find in the way of a story. I've got time to kill because there's another story brewing down the road for the following week. So I figure I'll scratch around this dusty patch and try and uncover *something*, just some small worm of an idea I might tease out and entertain myself with for a few days. And lo and behold there are worms everywhere. And the juiciest one comes presented on a platter! The moment I introduce myself to the store's proprietor she offers me her father's story, nay, *insists* I do the story of her father, who'd been one of the pioneers of the area. Furthermore she'll make *him* do it too, she says, putting us both on notice.

There's nothing self-serving about her bossiness. She loves her father and believes his story should be told; simple as that. All close families know this kind of blind loyalty. But unbeknown to me at that stage she also knows he's a fan of mine. (One of the diminishing few with faculties intact, I dare say, since dementia is surely eroding my fan base these days.) "We've tried to get him to tell his story before," she confides later, "but he wouldn't. Then when you turned up I knew if he was ever going to tell anyone it would be you. He loved you on television."

Of course this kind of flattery is always easy on the ears, and I'm certainly grateful when it facilitates my current work. But such a commission carries tremendous responsibility. To tell a man's story is to impose, to a lesser or greater degree, your own judgements on his life. Put simply you'll highlight what you find interesting, and skim over what you don't. And to tell the story of a man to someone who loved him is to accept disappointment as a likely response to your best efforts. For you'll never see the man in quite the same way they did, not in dimension or deed, fantasy or fact. Therefore the best I can usually offer is a hasty vignette, a snapshot taken by my own erring hand, hopefully carrying something of the essence of a life. And it's this inadequate portrait we must console ourselves with here, I'm afraid. (At least until we all get dementia and it no longer matters.)

The man in question enters through the back of the store and shakes my hand, smiling. He has a kind face – a term I've never been able to satisfactorily describe, incidentally, since it presents a different guise in every owner – and he wears large prescription glasses and a floppy white hat. He is about the same vintage as my own father and the similarity doesn't end there. He bears the stamp of humility I've seen in the Old Man at times, a dignified acceptance of things as they are as opposed to how he might have once wanted them to be. And I'm reminded of this because his daughter is now telling us how things will be, and insisting I do the same. I laugh and say I don't have her front, but he seems happy enough to oblige anyway, or at least knows better than to deny his daughter. So within ten minutes of meeting we're driving south to the ruins of a house he built forty years ago.

On the way he tells me he came to the Roper as a young man to hunt crocodiles with a mate.

"We used to harpoon them first," he explains. "Then depending on the size and the way they were, eventually you pulled them up alongside the boat and shot 'em and pulled them in. Occasionally they'd come back to life again in the boat, and you'd have your foot on the croc's head and suddenly they'd start moving and you'd have to shoot 'em again," he says, grinning, "But it was good fun."

Then they'd skin the crocs and send the cured hides to Darwin. He tells me the biggest croc they took was seventeen feet and eight inches long, with a pelt sixty-nine inches wide, but the big skins were more trouble than they were worth.

"The ones around ten foot were the best," he says. "They didn't use much salt, and you'd get the maximum money for them. And it was only a little bundle when it was dried up," he mimes holding something about as round as a basketball. "The big ones you couldn't even lift on your own. And they'd take a whole bag of salt."

Crocodile hunting was banned in the late sixties but he stayed on in the area and returned to his trade as a builder, which is how he came to build the St Vidgeons homestead.

"Back then the road out wasn't much better than a goat track, just two tracks in the sand. Took two days to get from Mataranka to The Bar," he tells me, referring to a 180 kilometre stretch between the Stuart Highway and Roper Bar that you can do in two hours these days.

"This road here used to flood regularly, and one time we corduroyed a section with logs to get through. So for a laugh my wife made up a sign, 'Hand-made road – Toll $10' and hung it on a tree. Some tourists believed it and turned around and went back!

"But the name stuck." He points out the "Toll Gate Creek" sign as we pass, chuckling at the recollection. A small legacy for future generations to barely notice as they rush by in their new four wheel drives.

For part of the drive the road runs parallel to the Roper River and he tells me about the Young Australian, the largest vessel to be shipwrecked in the Roper and the only known paddle steamer to come to grief in the Territory. At the time she was being used to tow smaller sailing ships upriver to unload supplies for the completion of the Overland Telegraph Line, the north-south communications wire that effectively connected Australia to the rest of the world. Because it was more expedient for supply ships to offload at Roper River than continue on to Port Darwin, a Construction Depot was established on the Roper. This enabled work on the central parts of the Line to be completed in time to meet the undersea section coming from Java, without incurring the late penalties written into the contract.

"We used to ski in the Roper as well," my guide tells me.

"What about the crocodiles?"

"Good incentive to stay up," he says, grinning, and for a moment I can see him as a young tear-away, night skiing up the river for kicks after a few grogs with the boys.

At first glance the old homestead looks like a Besser block construction on its way *up* rather than one on its way down to rubble. The blocks were all hand-made using local sand and gravel, and cement he trucked in from town, so it's not surprising they've stood up. Unguarded iron and timber doesn't last long in this country, though, and the roof, doors and windows have long ago been appropriated elsewhere. Even the electrical fittings have been stripped from the walls, and any timber remaining lays white ant ridden on the floor. Despite all this it's still clear this was once a substantial home, especially for such a remote area.

"How long did it take you to build?" I ask him.

"Oh, about three months, I think."

"Three months! You climbed into it then."

"Well, I had two Aboriginal helpers with me; they were pretty good. Only when the concrete mixer caught fire one day they bolted."

"How many people lived in the area then?"

"Well, there were about seven or eight hundred Aboriginals at the settlement there at Ngukurr, which used to be a mission in them days. There was also a supply camp for Aboriginals at the Police Station at Roper Bar."

"What about at Port Roper?"

"Nothing, there was nothing there at all. And I even got a letter from a school in New York one day addressed to the Mayor of Port Roper."

We both laugh at the thought. If you've ever seen Port Roper, even today, you'd understand. There's still nothing there, save a few Vietnamese crabbers and a crusty old barra fisherman who occasionally presides over his patch like an *unofficial* mayor, but I doubt he'd embrace official international duties.

Leaning out the open window of the old laundry we watch a flock of black cockatoos feeding on casuarina nuts, and the builder remembers a story.

"One day my wife and the kids were alone here, and she had a snake in the house. And see that rubble drain just there from the toilet? Well the snake went down that hole. And once before I'd told her the way to get a snake out of a hole was to put a bit of petrol down and light it. So she did that, and *whoomph*, the whole septic tank blew up."

"I hope nobody was sitting on the throne."

"No, the kids were all sitting on the kitchen table while she was out lighting petrol."

Still chuckling, he picks up a length of rotten timber.

"See this bit of wood? Forty-something years ago I had that in my hands. Several times, I suppose. Time goes," he says, and throws it back onto the floor. "The timber all came by boat from Queensland, which was the cheapest way to get anything in those days."

But he's no sentimentalist. As we keep wandering through the graffitied blockwork and knee high grass growing through cracks in the floor, I ask him if he thinks the ruins should be preserved as part of our history.

"No, I would put the bulldozer through it and level it out and be done with it."

He takes me down to the home billabong, where he once had a windmill pumping water up to the main tank above the homestead providing a permanent water supply. A boon so far from the river, no doubt, but he tells me the water was so rich in aquatica it wouldn't keep in the water bag; when the critters died they smelled and blocked up the canvass bags, so they were constantly washing them out.

"And we used to swim here," he says, looking out over the lily padded surface and remembering.

"No doubt there's crocs."

"Yeah there's crocs here."

"And mosquitos," I say, slapping one.

"And barramundi," he adds.

"The whole Territory experience in the one little duck pond."

Then he shows me what he calls the original Queensland Crossing* on the Hodgson River, where the Duracks drove their herds of cattle into the Territory and beyond back in the late 1800s. It's a natural rock shelf wide enough for two cars to pass comfortably if not smoothly, for it's pitted with deep, round sink holes drilled by rocks burrowing into the bedrock in the turbulence of a million wet season torrents. Downstream the volcanic boulders and slabs have been worn shiny by the waterflow, and many bear petroglyphs etched into their surface by the local inhabitants of an indeterminate age ago. My guide tells me he's brought scientists here to document the etchings, but remains sceptical of their findings. He draws my attention to a footprint on a large lump of long-cooled lava.

"One, two, three, four, five, six," he counts the toes. "Six toes. One, two, three, big mobs. And when the anthropologist from Melbourne University came here, he said that's a footprint made when the rock was still hot. And you can see his hand where he supported himself, and he pushed the lava out. Now there's a tall story for you."

We agree they must encourage fertile imaginations in universities these days and carry on inspecting the other etchings of bird tracks, picaninny footprints and sundry other shapes both recognisable and otherwise. And as we're moving around freely admiring these ancient Aboriginal artworks under a rude blue sky, I wonder how long it'll be before the tourist buses start turning up at even this out-of-the-way gallery. There are other significant Aboriginal sites

*I suspect one and the same as the crossing I've heard others refer to as Rocky Bar.

in the area, and enough white history to appeal to both camps. Presently it's still a pretty rough stretch of dirt between Roper Bar and Borroloola and there's certainly not much in the way of facilities, but with the ever-increasing traffic on the Savannah Way it's probably only a matter of time before whole of the Gulf is opened up to tourism. Christ knows there's nothing else likely to open it up.

But the builder won't be around to see it anyway. In recent years he's moved to live in gentler climes on the Atherton Tablelands in North Queensland. I ask him if he misses this country.

"Well, yes and no, but I'm much more comfortable where I am now."

But later as we turn for home he says about the only sentimental thing I heard him say the whole time.

"No," he qualifies apropos of nothing I heard or said, "I had some great times here."

FANCY PANTS AND CHRISTMAS TREE

They call him Fancy Pants and he swears so much I had the bleep going almost constantly through the video story. The reason they call him Fancy Pants is because sometimes he wears hot pink bicycle shorts to work. He's a grader driver by occupation, and the bloke who told me about him said he nearly fell over the first time he saw Fancy Pants climb out of the cabin resplendent in pink shorts and shirt knotted at the midriff *a la* Peter Allen. "It's not what you expect out here in the bush," he told me. I suggested he might have been hot, to which he replied enthusiastically, "Oh he was *hot* all right." But he couldn't quite articulate what he thought he was hot for.

When I meet Fancy Pants he is modestly dressed in a black Jacky Howe singlet, black stretch boxer shorts and thongs. The shorts could well be underpants, I suppose, but I don't pursue the point. He wears a peaked brown cap on a head full of long blonde hair, with sunnies, John Holmes moustache and gold neck chain for accessories. His bare shoulders are brown and bony and the overall effect is certainly original, but I don't consider it outrageous. I do ask him at one stage if he'll put the pink pants on for me but he just looks at me suspiciously. Again I don't pursue it.

His mate is far more traditionally dressed – if there is such a thing as a standard for grader drivers – in a navy and fluoro-yellow work shirt, navy shorts and thongs. He wears a sweat-stained brown felt hat to shade his already suntanned face, which is never far from cracking a grin, and his features are defined and expressive, especially his eyebrows, which he often knits together in the middle of his forehead like the uppermost branches of a Christmas tree.

Each is his own man, but together they form part of the mighty outback corrugation corps, those selfless souls who spend great chunks of their lives on lonely roads, scraping the menace from their surface so we can enjoy them at least for a month or two, before they deteriorate into rutted hell once more. Okay, so I'm getting a little carried away, but I'm not a fan of corrugations. I ask Fancy Pants what causes them.

"Just springs bouncing, traffic going too xxxxing fast," he says. "That's what causes them most, the speed. You watch them tourists flying past after a road's been graded, they sit on about a hundred and xxxxing twenty kays an hour, and all you can see is the xxxxing tyres going boom boom boom boom boom," he illustrates by rapidly smacking one palm down on the other, "and their boat carriers or xxxxing trailers they're pulling, you can see the wheels bouncing up and down.

"If it's wet," he continues, "the traffic'll pack it down; it'll last a lot longer. But when it's dry it corrugates quicker.

"The Works Department here – we call 'em Works and Jerks – they dug some corrugations out with a backhoe. Thirty metres they go down. From the xxxxing traffic, going too fast. And trucks, they're the worst."

He tells me there is no solution, and recalls a test they did with a rubber compound mixed with gravel out on the Hermannsburg road one time, which was supposed to last forever. In twelve months it was xxxxed. He says.

He takes me for a ride in the cabin. It's noisy and dusty, especially with the door open to film the action, but there's something comforting about watching that big blade cutting all those corrugations down to size. We bounce along gently as the landscape slides past, Fancy Pants concentrating on the road ahead, left hand on the steering wheel, right hand on one of the four black control knobs.

"What's the enemy out here? Dust?" I ask him.

"Tourists," he corrects without hesitation. "Dust you get used to."

"Why do tourists get up your nose?"

"Well they go too fast, they dust you when they pass, they don't slow down for signs, especially Victorians and New South Wales xxxxs. They're the worst of the xxxxing lot."

Christmas Tree agrees about the tourists being the biggest worry, but doesn't discriminate between the states. When I ask him about them it's one of the few times he doesn't laugh in response.

"Oh yeah, some of them are bloody idiots."

"You haven't hit one?"

"No. Went close a couple of times, though."

"What about posts? I see you have to do some fancy cutting in at times. Ever take a post out?"

"Oh, yeah," he says, grinning but not elaborating.

I laugh and don't pursue it, which tactic is fast-becoming my modus operandi for this story. I'm talking to them separately so neither knows what the other is saying. But they're still both loyal enough not to shop their mate. Or savvy enough, not forgetting it's being recorded. Christmas Tree tells me he shares a camp with Fancy Pants but won't be drawn into divulging any of his fashion secrets, apart from saying he likes to keep himself well-groomed. I ask him who does the cooking.

"We cook for ourselves, yeah."

"Who's the better cook?"

"Oh, that's hard to say," he laughs. "You get some pretty rough meals. Especially after a few beers."

They both work for the one contractor and as well as camping together they also work in tandem, with one grader taking the cut directly behind the leader when they grade a road. Fancy Pants tells me they cover around twenty kilometres this way, whereas the old government quota for two graders used to be less than half that.

"But they were xxxxing hopeless," he says.

"Is it all contract work now?"

"Yeah, has been for years. But the government used to have their own crews. But they was xxxxing useless. Wouldn't do two kilometres a day, some of 'em, never mind five or six."

"So does the life suit you out in the bush?"

"Yeah, it's magic," he says. "Good life out bush. Meet a lot of good people, see a lot of good country, good rivers, camping spots."

"Can't see yourself moving back to town?"

"No, hate town."

In contrast, Christmas Tree's relationship with civilisation is a little more complicated.

"What's the worst part of the job?" I ask him.

"Oh, being away from home."

"What's the best part of the job?

"Being in the bush."

"So it's a bit each way then."

"Yeah, after a few days in there I want to get back out here."

"What about your missus? Is she keen to send you back out?"

"Oh yeah, I think so, yeah," he says, grinning enigmatically.

I laugh and don't pursue it.

IN THE PURPLE

Iron ore. The commonest ore in the world. It's everywhere. Just lying around ready to be picked up and sold. Brazil has been picking it up for years. Ditto India, China, Canada, Sweden, South Africa, Ukraine and let's not forget Australia. And that's not counting the countries where they've got it but haven't quite got around to picking it up yet, like Bolivia, Peru and just about any other developing nation you can think of where it's possible to stub your toe on a rock. Asia's buying and everyone wants a piece of the action.

The Pilbara is the big player in Australia. It produces over 90% of our iron ore amounting to roughly 15% of the world's needs and making us one of the largest producers of iron ore in the world. Incidentally we also produce about a third of the world's coal, so if you've been in the habit of defending Australia's role in greenhouse gas emissions on the grounds of limited contribution perhaps you should think again; we may not be big users, but as dealers we're up there with the Corleones. And the same applies to uranium.

But I digress. I'm talking about iron ore. And I'm talking about iron ore because I'm at an iron ore exploration camp. We spend a lot of money on exploration in this country, mostly because we're afraid our premium reserves will run out in 50 years if we continue to mine them at the current rate. And this, in spite of the assertion Tom Price* made in the sixties, that trying to calculate how much ore there is in the Pilbara is like trying to calculate how much air

*The American geologist who was one of the first to recognise the potential of mining iron ore in the Hammersley ranges. He died before his belief was fully substantiated and they named the town in his honour.

there is. Crikey! Does this mean even the air is a finite resource?

Yet I'm not anti-mining any more than I am anti-breathing. I do have some issues with our cavalier approach to mining, true, but that's just capitalism doing its thing, right? And I do have a few concerns about how little of the *real* gains stay in Australia, but again, surely that's merely capitalism dancing on the world stage. And while I'm on a roll I admit I'm also sceptical about growth-at-all-costs business models, excessive Western consumption and the disingenuousness of governments publicly touting control of an industry they're desperately courting behind closed doors. But then, that's just capitalism hiding under the coattails of trusty old democracy, is it not? And what could be more wholesome than that?

No, I'm not against mining, because the mines aren't to blame for any of this. Nor the miners. It's us. We want, they provide. If we didn't want, they wouldn't provide and the cycle would be arrested, or at least slowed. We can rail all we like but until we stop consuming they won't stop producing. And as long as we have big business and governments encouraging us to spend to keep economies growing, we won't stop consuming and they won't stop producing. Simple, but true. You can bet your mortgage on it.

So I've come to an exploration camp to see how that cog slots into this seductive cycle of supply and demand. And I've told the operators I want to get right down into the engine room of the thing, to the pulsing heart and soul of the matter. To wit, the kitchen. I've heard good things about this cook, and I want to get her slant on life in a mining camp. As it happens I'm getting two angles for the price of one.

To begin with the camp's a more temporary affair than I imagined, not much more than a handful of tents, caravans and containers all given over to living quarters of one kind or another, scattered over about an acre of red soil woodland on the Towns River flats in Gulf Country, Northern Territory. At a guess it looks like it could handle about forty or fifty workers, and every one of them comes under the motherly scrutiny of the camp cook.

She a jolly, brown-skinned, middle-aged woman with bright eyes and frizzy, short-cropped hair. When I meet her she's busy preparing a luncheon spread for a party of government mining officials due to arrive for a tour of the facilities. The kitchen occupies most of the space in a medium-sized caravan and looks functional and new.

"So do you find yourself playing Agony Aunt?" I ask her as she wraps a sushi roll at one of the benches.

"Yeah," she laughs warmly. "Of course. Especially to my husband."

Her husband is the camp's maintenance/handy/everything man, and from what I can gather they only accept postings where they can be together. When I tell him his wife reckons he takes more looking after than the boys he laughs and agrees that's likely, because he's a naughty boy. They're an amusing double act.

But they take the business of looking after "their boys" seriously, and it's clearly appreciated. When I ask the boys how the tucker is the responses are heartfelt and clear: "Bloody good," says one; "Very good, better than at home," says another; and "Tucker's fantastic, mate. [She] does a great job, [He] helps out, and it's all good," says a bloke who tells me he's been working in mining camps for much of his life. I ask a dozen more and there's no exception to the positive feedback.

"This is a family unit," the naughty one tells me. "They're going to spend more time with [us], and their workmates, than they are with their loved ones at home. So for the months that we're here at this camp, we are these people's family. We live, breathe, care for them, make sure they've got all their toiletries stuff, make sure the toilets are clean, they get the best of food, plenty of water, do the right thing and have clean clothes on."

"What about bush safety?" I ask.

"I'm always on their case about that," he says. "I don't like to see them in shorts."

"You don't find a man in shorts attractive?"

He laughs, "No, not at all."

Back in the kitchen the cook is still rolling sushi and I remind her that the video I'm shooting is going to be broadcast in Asia. She laughs and feigns concern, but she's too competent to be self-conscious. She tells me she's been cooking all her life and even thought about opening her own restaurant, but doubts she'd cope with the tedium of following the same menu night after night. "Out here you've got to improvise," she says. And utilise what you've got, it seems. She offers me some lightly battered, wild-caught Roper River barramundi fresh from the pan and it's as good as any barra I've had and I've had plenty.

"Is there more to it than just making sure they're fed, do you think?" I ask.

"Oh I think so. I like to think I'm mum. And my husband's a good listener. *And* a good talker, as anyone'll tell you. But we're mum and dad of the camp."

"Do they call you Mum?"

"No, they haven't yet. Oh, actually, yes, they have. A couple have," she laughs.

It's a warm touch to a harsh work environment. I'm taken out to see the drilling onsite and as expected it's dusty and dirty and noisy and hot. And unexpectedly purple! Iron ores come in an array of colours from yellow and orange through to brown and grey.* This deposit is so purple it leaves your hands the colour of mulberry stains if you handle it.

While still in feasibility mode there are strong signs this site will turn into a working mine. The ore is high grade with a very low phosphorous content, it's closer to the coast than any other iron ore body in Australia, and much of the ore is on the surface and requires no pre-strip before mining ore begins.

"It'll be like harvesting wheat," one of the bosses tells me. "I think it's got the potential to be a new iron ore province in Australia." A purple province.

But it's no accident this is about us underpopulated as any region in the land. In the wet season these areas get isolated by flooded rivers for months on end, and in the dry season it's so parched and challenging that you soon find yourself wishing for the wet. It's easy to see why these blokes appreciate a homely touch back at camp.

"Does the mood of the camp affect you here?" I ask the cook. "Do you sense whether they're doing well out there?"

"Oh yeah. You can't help it, it's…"

"You become part of the family?"

"'Course you do, 'course you do. And it's just like any other family, when somebody's upset or they're not happy, you feel it, you feel it."

---

*Iron ore is not a specific element, but rather a variety of rocks and minerals rich in iron oxides, which vary in colour depending on the host body, the purity, the degree of oxidation and weathering, etc.

BUSH FAREWELL

In the cool of the Limmen River morning a helicopter flies low over the water and a man leans out to shake the remains of his friend from a plastic urn. "Get out you old bastard," he says just to say something, anything to give the moment weight – but not too much, not too sombre now; this is the Australian bush, after all, where even grief is taken dry.

Lining the riverbank a small crowd watches respectfully as the ashes trail from the neck of the urn, dusting the sides of the chopper and the tops of the trees as they drift down to the water. Then a young girl breaks the mood with a squeal as she realises she has dust in her eyes. Someone laughs and tells her it's good luck to get a dead man's ashes in your eyes but she looks doubtful. The crowd relaxes and murmurs follow the chopper across the river where the remaining remains are cast over a fishing boat abandoned in the mud. The empty urn tumbles into the river and the breeze scoots it off into the mangroves, like a man alive would move if he were dropped in that river full of crocs. A white hat is tossed onto the boat. Then the chopper does another circuit while the man pours a beer over the ashes, except the beer is partly frozen and the best he can do is shake a few drops from the can. Chuckles acknowledge the *faux pas* and a sense of appropriate closure settles over the crowd as the helicopter departs; it has been a worthy good bye.

The crowd is made up mostly of bush men, hardened drinkers and rogues many of them, along with a few tourists who've wandered over from the fishing camp. Most have made a long journey to be here to pay their respects. Yet not for this lot any showy displays of melancholy; before the chopper has wound down the crack and fizz of beer cans opening signals their customary intentions. Now the tongues will be lubricated for the stories to flow, the unreliable accounts of a man's feats, follies and foibles that serve as evidence of a life well lived, and therefore a life well known.

The helicopter pilot soon joins the throng and remembers a time his old friend went missing, presumed dead. He spent days flying over harsh country in search, eventually finding him sitting under a tree by a billabong in the middle of nowhere, reading a book.

"It was a thing, all right," he says, using the impersonal 'it' with great fondness. "It had half a beast hung up in a tree over there, a pig that musta come in for the beast shot dead underneath it – it was doing all right for itself no worries – and when I climbed out of the chopper it didn't get up, just looked down its nose at me through these little reading glasses and said, 'About time you showed up.'"

The urn bearer is also our host, a congenial pro fisherman with a wild ginger beard and moustache and the ruddy complexion of someone who exposes fair skin to the elements. I spoke with him before the chopper went up and he expressed some reservations about hanging out on the skid to scatter the ashes.

"So were you pleased with how it went up there?" I ask him now. "You didn't feel like you were going to fall?"

"No, I didn't feel like it at all. I felt like jumping out, not falling." He laughs and takes a pull on his beer.

"And what was the significance of the boat wreck?"

"Oh, he done a bit of sea time with me on that boat, so…" he trails off, finishing the sentence with a narrowing of the eyes, a look away. "But that old urn didn't want to stay in there, eh?" he recovers quickly. "Straight up the mangroves."

"We were gonna shoot a donkey or a horse so we could make some pocket steak," jokes another, "then stick his ashes in that and feed it to the crocodiles, 'cause he *feared* crocodiles," he laughs. Then he makes a point of assuring me he was a good mate while he was alive, lest I get the wrong impression.

It's an interesting thing to be an outsider at a wake, to have your only window to the dead thrown open by those who want the life to fill the gap. You can't ever join their club now – membership is closed – but they will invite you in as a *bona fide* guest, as a witness.

And so I listen to the stories being shared, along with the younger men deferring to the older men. There is a hierarchy here, an order of merit determined by closeness of bond and shared experience. After family, being a contemporary assumes the highest rung on the mourning ladder. It's as if everyone understands the need to affirm life through the window of death, and the closer to the window the better the view. Both ways, perhaps.

The women, too, are taking a back seat at this table, though whether that's because the dead man had few significant women in his life at the end, or because women do their mourning differently it's hard to say. One woman who knew him, though not well, she said, admits to a tinge of sadness. But that's the only obvious sign of sentimentality I see.

Mostly it's the predictable, "Grab us another beer, mate; that's what he'd 'a' wanted," or "Remember when the bastard did this, or that?" as another Aussie soul is committed to the past by those left to endure the present.

Yet unpredictable things do happen at funerals and wakes. I don't know if it's the heightened awareness of our own mortality or just the unstable mix of alcohol, emotion and a whole lot of people who wouldn't otherwise socialise, but I've seen some wild stuff go down with the dead. Fighting between the best of friends, sex between the oddest of pairings, acute breakdowns in the stablest of characters. Funny how the events specifically designed to bring humans closer together – weddings, funerals, Christmas – have the most potential to blow up.

But there's nothing too volatile about this one. Morning eases into afternoon and the crowd thins. Mud crabs are cooked in a pot over the fire as kites wheel and cry overhead. The house chooks scratch around in the dry soil for something they may have overlooked last time around and on the end of his chain a dog sleeps with one ear cocked. The women move indoors to talk while the men settle in for a session of drinking and bullshitting outside, and healthy brown kids with big white smiles try out both camps before deciding it just feels better with Mum. It's not really a day for kids.

And somewhere along the way I fall off the wagon and join in. I can't really say why, since I'm still drying out from Darwin and I'm normally a fairly disciplined unit, but I do anyway. First it's a gold can or two, then I remember a warm bottle of black home brew waiting for me in Claude, then someone produces a bottle of *green* home-made grappa, God help me. The rest is predictable, of course, the path well-trod, but eventually, inevitably, I succumb to the weight of the gold and the black and the green. And in the heat of that Limmen River afternoon I lay down in the shade of a tree and close my eyes.

TURTLE NIGHTS

The most memorable thing I learn about big turtles that night is how crocodiles sometimes pick them off while they're laying their eggs in the sand. Tough school; nature. But it must be an exhilarating thing to see a four metre croc walk up the beach and grab a sixty kilogram turtle then carry back it to the sea in its mouth. Especially if you're at the nest counting eggs at the time.

This doesn't happen to me, I hasten to add, but from the moment I hear the story I can't stop imagining what I'd do if it does. Between us we've got a camera, a torch and a quad bike to defend ourselves with. I workshop a couple of valiant scenarios but they all end with me leaving the scene as fast as I can on the quad bike, *a la* Lord Jim*.

As you've probably gathered I'm shooting a turtle story. I'm on West Island, one of the Sir Edward Pellew group of islands in the southwestern Gulf of Carpentaria, and I'm with a group of people stumbling around in the dark collecting data on the breeding habits of the Flatback Turtle. Some are scientists from the Northern Territory's Department of Natural Resources, Environment, the Arts and Sport – surely the most diverse portfolio in politics – some are local Lianthawirriyarra Sea Rangers and their families, and I think there are also a few student volunteers getting some field experience to supplement their zoology studies. I say "think"

---

*Lord Jim was the principle character in Joseph Conrad's book of the same name, who deserted his duties as Captain of his sinking ship in favour of saving himself in the only life raft. Unfortunately for him the ship didn't sink after all, and Lord Jim spent the rest of the book trying to reconcile his unforgivable act of cowardice.

because it's so dark I can't see anything but crocodile shadows at the moment. We're supposed to be looking for tracks of turtles going up to lay, but how on earth we're expected to see them I've no clue.

I needn't have worried; they're not subtle. It's not like tracking Jerboa in the desert (which I've never done, but I can imagine). It's a Flatback track we find first, the most prevalent turtle here. They also get occasional visits from some of the other six varieties of marine turtles found in Australia, but this part of the Gulf is known mainly for Flatback and Green Turtles, and West island is specifically recognised as a Flatback rookery. (Incidentally, these waters are also considered one of the most significant dugong breeding grounds in the world.)

A little way up the tracks we find the turtle flippering her bulk across the sand with surprising agility. Although she does grind to a halt when the team sets upon her back to take carapace measurements and fix tags and whatever else they do while I'm looking over my shoulder for crocodiles. Then we follow her up to the drier sand above high water mark where she'll lay her eggs. I'm shooting what I can of this moveable feast, but I have to be careful not to confuse the turtle with light because she'll follow its source wherever it leads, and since I'm following her it's best she doesn't follow me.

Once she finds a suitable location she clears the dry sand away with all four flippers, then digs a chamber for the eggs with her curiously delicate hind flippers. They look like leathery old chicken wings and move like the hands of a concert pianist. The chamber is about half a metre down and hollowed out enough to hold fifty or so eggs, which are round and semi-soft to withstand the drop. When she's finished laying she fills the hole with sand, gives it a thorough pat down with her hind flippers, then heads back to sea for another couple of years. It's a bravura performance and in any other forum she'd get flowers, at least. But here all she gets is her nest dug up so the team can count the eggs even before she's out of sight.

Turtle conservation is a sensitive issue in this country. It evokes a high degree of emotion, even to the point of counter-productivity. That afternoon the supervising scientist agreed to let me film his team in action only on the proviso his department could approve the story before it went to air. They get more than their share of people objecting to every minor scientific intervention, so understandably they like to keep it manageable.

"Really we're looking at monitoring sea turtles right across the Northern Territory," he tells me. "And most of the coastline of the NT is indigenous-owned, so to monitor sea turtles effectively we have to work in partnership with indigenous rangers and communities."

"Are the countrymen seriously looking at turtles as a sustainable resource now?" I ask, hoping my doubts aren't too obvious.

"This is a Flatback Turtle project so they're quite different to the ones they normally harvest. They normally harvest Green Turtles for meat, but they'll harvest eggs of all species, so Flatbacks are included in that.

"But part of the ranger programs that are occurring all across northern Australia, the rangers and the communities are continually looking at better resource management, and we all have different ways of doing it."

Nicely put. But I still don't want to come back as a turtle.

There's fifty-eight eggs in the nest, random samples of which are measured and weighed, before the clutch is returned to the chamber and the hole re-filled. Most of the work is done by the

Lianthawirriyarra crew, with the kids in particular encouraged to get involved. A pink ribbon is left trailing from the hole to mark the spot. I soon find out why.

We stumble on through the dark night. There's no sign of a moon yet and I imagine the cover lessens the chance of the turtles being taken by a crocodile. Then I remember seeing a David Attenborough story where crocs were plucking leaping mullet from the air in the dead of night; what chance a lumbering old turtle? For that matter what chance a lumbering old me? I take two steps sideways and put another of my colleagues between me and the water.

Someone has found the pink ribbon from a spent nest. The hatchlings have probably hit the water last night, so now it's the team's job to dig up the nest and tally the hatch-rate.

"Usually out of fifty eggs you might have forty-five that have hatched and got away," the scientist tells me. "You might have two or three unfertilised or undeveloped eggs, and you might have two or three that have half-developed but have died along the way."

And so it proves, although the volunteers seem a little less enthusiastic about diving into this nest; in the six weeks the eggs have been incubating the infertile and unborn have had plenty of time to go rotten, and it's not the most pleasant of tasks.

Far and away the most impressive field work I saw that night, though, was a laparoscopy, performed on an adult turtle to determine whether she'd bred before.

"It's important because it gives us a look into the future," explains the scientist as he secures the flippers of a turtle they've upended on a wheelbarrow. "If we have no new recruits... then it looks pretty bleak for the population, because once all the older females die off we've got no new ones coming through. Likewise if we had too many new recruits it could be something that's happening to the older population."

To perform the operation a small incision is made in the soft skin beside the tail flippers and a viewing tube is inserted into the body cavity so the ovarian follicles can be scrutinised. If scarring is obvious then she's bred before, if there's no scarring it's likely she's a newcomer. In this case it looks as though she's a first-time breeder, which is good news. Again the Lianthawirriyarra rangers are encouraged to get involved in the process and it's heartwarming to see such a healthy collaboration between science and tradition.

We don't finish till well after midnight and it's a strangely satisfying trudge back to camp; I suspect mostly because it feels like the data we've gathered might actually be of some use in the larger picture, but I'm also quite pleased I didn't get taken by a crocodile.

The next morning I rise early and return to the scene of the previous night's labours and I'm surprised at how few signs remain. What was exciting theatre under lights last night has now been reduced to a few sets of tracks already being washed away by the tide. Walking along the pristine shoreline I notice a container ship sitting just offshore waiting to be filled with zinc from the McArthur River Mine, and I wonder what will become of these quiet backwaters when they start shipping iron ore as well. And between this growing threat, marauding crocodiles and hungry countrymen it's suddenly very clear to me these turtles are going to need all the help they can get.

WET WET

They're stocking up for an early wet season in the Gulf this year.

"Early and long," Kevin, one of the regulars at Karumba's Animal Bar tells me. "In 2009 we got cut off for two months. Beer got very expensive because they had to bring it in by barge. The government subsidised food to be flown in, but not the grog."

We agree only a government lacking compassion would do such a thing. This is country where driving distances are measured in cans of beer consumed, and wet season flood-ins by the pallet.

A local fisherman with a broad smile and the nickname Box tells me he normally orders in half a pallet to see them through the wet, but this season they're ordering a full pallet.

"All the signs are pushing to a big wet this year," he says. "The build-up's early, the hermit crabs have been getting way up into the trees, the mud crabs are carrying eggs already. They must know something."

Kyra from the Barramundi Discovery Centre agrees.

"My girls have all spawned early," she tells me as she dangles a pilchard in the water for a twenty-five kilogram breeder called Glenora. The barramundi glides up lazily and considers the offering before hoovering it down with a whump and a splash and turning back to the depths of the tank.

"Normally at this time we'd be turning the heaters on to get them interested, but they've been working hard all night, haven't you my darlings?" she says dividing her attention equally between me and the fish, although I must say I don't get offered a pilchard.

"Any other signs you've noticed," I ask. "Ants, birds?"

"Yeah, the ants have been busy climbing trees. So unless they've run out of room on the ground there must be a reason. But I'm not the one to ask about birds." And I'm thinking that's the end of that line of thought when she catches me off guard and hollers over her shoulder, "Raymond, any birds doing anything weird! We're after sure signs of an early wet. Bit of bullshit for the people."

"Well I've got six dead chooks in the freezer, how about that?" comes the helpful reply from an unseen Raymond.

"Oh, and the tourists!" Kyra remembers. "They cleared out early this year. Too hot for them."

I drive about ten kilometres north of the port to Karumba Point where most of the tourists stay and it's true the caravan parks are all but empty. One of the parks' permanent residents, another Kevin, thinks they might be right about the early wet predictions, also citing ants as the indicator. "They've moved in!" he says, pointing to his caravan. I ask if he's making friends with them or giving them the chemical treatment. "A bit of both," he answers, his face a droll portrait of evil.

Back at the port the Animal Bar has attracted a few more clients and John is upping the ante to a three pallet wet. "I reckon it's going to be a very big wet and we'll be cut off for two or three months," he says confidently, almost triumphantly. "The ants have been active for a while now, which is always a good sign, and these corellas refuse to leave town." He's referring to a wild bunch of corellas that have come too late and stayed too long, now getting on everyone's nerves with their noisy nonsense.

Yet at Normanton, seventy kilometres inland from Karumba, people are far more circumspect. You wouldn't think a town with a purple pub, a pink cafe and a bright green butchery would be conservative, but they're doing caution with reckless abandon here.

A group of men that gathers most mornings at the Top Servo and likes to be known as the Information Centre offers nothing in the way of useful information. I admit I may have made a blunder asking why some locals refer to them as the CWA, but they seem very suspicious of my motives. The most definite response I get to the wet season question is a grumpy "Nobody knows".

Likewise the nice lady at the post office who takes the weather readings at the airport tells me she hasn't noticed any pattern forming yet either way, and doesn't feel she's been around long enough to comment in any case.

It isn't till I'm on my way out of Normanton that I find anyone prepared to commit.

Firstly Pam who's visiting from Karumba tells me she's backing an early wet because the crocodiles have started eating people on the streets; a claim supported by her fisherman husband, Al – one in every three men in Karumba is either a fisherman or a Kevin – who lends some credibility to the banter by adding the crocodiles are also nesting earlier.

But the last word must go to Stella McNab, who after 87 years of watching the seasons come and go in Normanton is the closest I'm ever going to get to an expert on the matter. Stella walks from the supermarket wrestling her trolley, looking very smart in a pink skirt and blouse beneath a straw boater with a white satin sash. Though dainty she doesn't appear frail, and her face has been kindly treated. When I suggest a photograph she fusses and says she makes a poor subject, but she is wrong about that much. I take the picture and ask the question.

"No, it's not going to be an early wet," she says going against trend, narrowing her shining grey eyes slightly. "I follow the moon. When I grew up my father was the saddler and taxi driver here and I learned from all the old bushmen. And there's no ring around the moon yet.

"But I live just over there, and anyone who comes to visit gets a cup of tea and banana fritters. With home made jam and chutney," she remembers.

And that'll do me for a plan whatever the weather decides to do.

A THOUSAND
GOOD REASONS

At about this point in the trip Claude broke a leg. I'd been cajoling him along for the previous thousand kilometres or so – okay, I'm lying: I've been nursing the bastard since I got him, but usually for nothing serious enough to halt his progress – when he broke a torsion bar. For the uninitiated a torsion bar is a sprung steel rod used in lieu of springs or coils to support a load, in this case Claude's front end. The only other thing you need to know about torsion bars is they never break. A bloke told me that only the other week. "You'll never snap one of those," he said, looking at me like I was some kind of paranoid loon for even asking the question. "They suspend bridges with that steel."

Regrettably Claude doesn't care for reputations and he snapped the bar like a twig half-way between Karumba and Normanton. Went off with a bang so loud I thought I'd been shot. But as soon as I climbed down from the cabin I knew what was wrong. Nose down and leaning to one side there was no mistaking it; not a bridge in sight and Claude had busted a torsion bar.

Needless to say this caused a change of plan. You can't drive buses without suspension: they ride very poorly indeed. I still had twenty stories to shoot that I was hoping to find up on the Cape before the rains came, but now they'd have to wait till I made a pit stop. And on that front my options were limited. Mt Isa was 500 kilometres south, and while I knew of a good diesel fitter there it probably wasn't the best place to be servicing a mechanical unicorn. Cairns was 200 kilometres further but at least I'd be nearer the action if parts became a problem. I pointed Claude due east and winced at every bump.

Cairns proved a good choice. The available skill level is pretty high and overall it's not as avaricious as most capital cities. Even so, by the time I'd worked through the usual list of things to do when something major needs attention – see below* – I'd spent most of my inheritance and fathered six children. Okay, I'm exaggerating: there was no inheritance. But I did have a lot of fun trying to find another torsion bar. The ex-Japan price was a heart attack and I refused to order one on principle. Then after ringing every bus wrecker in the country only to learn the torsion bar in a 2WD Coaster isn't compatible with the 4WD – the 2WD bar is heavier, would you believe (probably to allow the off-road suspension more flex, but I thought it was a conspiracy at the time) – I had to swallow my pride and order the ex-Japan part anyway. In the meantime I got a very good welder to repair the broken rod – as a stopgap measure only, since there isn't a welding rod forged in hell that can match sprung steel – and got back underway.

As you can imagine all this took time, and if my friends in Karumba thought it was a risky proposition attempting Cape York *before* I hit Cairns it was now bordering on treacherous. While the monsoon trough is relatively easy to monitor and therefore factor into your travel plans, at this time of year isolated storm cells can

---

*Repair the throttle control unit, ditto the 4WD actuator, the transmission relay switch and a gaping hole in the roof, as well as treat Claude to a full service, new brake pads and diagnose the vanishing power issue, which turned out to be a shattered compressor fan in the turbocharger caused by gas entering the turbo as a liquid and crystallising. There were other things too but I'll spare us all the pain.

build-up and cut off river crossings overnight, and the Cape is riddled with river crossings. Common sense dictated I give up on the idea and head south.

As it happened I was right out of common sense by that stage and I took the Burke Development Road west. I wanted to take a look at a river crossing I'd heard about where the locals charge a retrieval fee of a thousand dollars per stranded vehicle. They call it the Koolatah Crossing and it fords the Mitchell River at Dunbar Station, offering about the only decent shortcut from the Gulf to the Cape. Providing you make it, of course. The very pleasant lady at Dunbar tells me they used to charge a bargain basement five hundred dollars but they were still getting too much work so they jacked the price up. And still people take it on and pay the money.

At first glance it looks benign enough. Though wide from bank to bank the approaches are gentle, there's a bit of sand but nothing low tyre pressures couldn't handle, and the channel seems an imminently do-able proposition. Indeed it presents a very pleasant vista and certainly not the sort of place you'd immediately associate with disaster.

Then you start looking beyond the welcome smile and see the teeth. That pretty sand is river sand, soft and dry enough to swallow you to the axles without spinning a wheel. And the water may not be more than a metre deep and thirty wide but it is running strong. And isn't this giant saltwater crocodile country?

I remember the story the lady at Dunbar Station told me about the German backpackers who got stuck in the middle of the crossing overnight. In the morning they found them locked in the cabin of their vehicle with towels covering the windows, "So the crocodiles couldn't see us," they explained. And why wouldn't a couple of tourists from Europe imagine our crocs could open car doors? Our stingrays kill national treasures and our dingoes take babies from tents, after all.*

I walk around, sizing things up. There's no way I'm taking Claude through; even with the turbo functioning I wouldn't attempt it without backup. The Mitchell has a catchment area about the size of Tasmania and any decent storm upstream could easily make flood debris of anything caught dawdling here. And overhead there are certainly signs of instability developing. But I still need some action for the video story. I need some other fool to have a shot. Just not this fool.

Then I see him. He looks a dandy in a Panama hat, blue shirt and navy shorts with white socks and sandshoes, and he's approaching from the far side with a clipboard in his hand, apparently doing a reccy of the crossing before he attempts it. I see his 4WD parked on the other bank, doors open and motor probably idling to keep his engine warm, although it's too far away to hear. He spots me and quickens his pace, obviously coming over to ask my opinion. Oh boy I've got a live one here! I figure this guy will not only have a crack but he's odds-on to get stuck in the process.

Disappointingly, though, it turns out he's surveying the riverbed for a low level crossing Main Roads intend to start building immediately. He's got no intention of having a shot in spite of my kind offer to film him in action. We have a chat across the channel and I draw his attention to the looming black clouds, telling him

---

*In 2006 Steve Irwin was speared by a stingray while filming one of his internationally acclaimed wildlife documentaries. And in 1980 baby Azaria Chamberlain disappeared from her tent in a campground at Uluru never to be seen again; after initial skepticism, it's now widely accepted a dingo was responsible. See footnote page 101 for more details.

many of the locals are predicting an early wet, which would surely interrupt their plans. He scoffs at the idea, claiming he never takes much notice of weather forecasts, especially from fanciful amateurs.

"I'm inclined to agree with you," I say. "I used to be a weatherman, you see. And I heard it every year: 'It's going to be a big wet, early wet, late wet, dry wet, long wet, short wet.' All in the same year I might add."

In short, what would they know?

I leave him to get on with his work and turn Claude around so we can get on with ours. Within ten minutes the sky blackens and fat drops of rain start hitting the windscreen so hard they sound like stones. Within half an hour the red dirt road is a slick of shimmering water and the rain has eased to a steady roar. I keep driving because I'm not game to pull off the road, and when I do finally make camp I choose the hardest ground I can find and still only just get out in the morning. Even once I reach the bitumen I'm still not out of the woods, as one by one the roads behind me are cut off by rising floodwaters. I barely make it through Queensland before an area larger than the size of Germany is underwater, or so the media reports tell us. It turns out to be the start of one of the wettest summers on record, with numerous cyclones and widespread flooding across three states and one territory, resulting in significant loss of life and billions of dollars worth of damage to property and livestock.

Like I said, what would they know?

EPIL●GUE

People hit the road for all sorts of reasons, for all sorts of results.

Some set off to see Australia and are satisfied to come home with a bundle of happy snaps and a cherished store of memories. Others dig a little deeper and perhaps work as they go, settling in to communities for short spells and getting to know a bit about the land and the people who live in it. Still more start off travelling and find themselves permanent fixtures somewhere without knowing quite how it happened. There's no right or wrong way to do it; it's all there for us to discover, understand and enjoy as we see fit.

Yet I fear in spite of the increased number of us travelling locally, the gulf continues to widen between urban and rural Australia, the city and the bush. We simply don't know what goes on out there anymore, and frankly I wonder if we really care. The bush is no longer relevant to the vast majority of Australians, beyond providing fodder for the occasional reality TV show or grim news story, or as a vague and grossly idealised notion of the Outback as our marketeers and promoters would have us imagine it.

Even our tourism bodies charged with the responsibility of selling the country seem at odds with the realities at times, so afraid are they of offending the consumer that they stage manage and air-brush the life out of anything too 'authentic'. For the consumer is everything, these days, and the product merely something to be shaped and styled according to market demands.

If Karl Marx's opiate for the masses was religion*, ours is now consumerism, and in less than fifty years we've turned even the bush into a consumable. And in doing so we've lost any real connection with it.

The failure of my two friends in this adventure – The Torso and my Big City Girl – to find any comfort out there would appear a case in point. Yes there were personal issues involved, but these two people were so clearly misplaced in the bush I might as well have had them to join me for a road trip on the moon. And yet in the city, on familiar turf, the relationships were tenable.

Of course it could be argued that urbanisation is the tide that must be taken at the flood**, and if losing touch with the bush is the result then so be it. But this can't be helping the very real skill shortage being faced in agricultural Australia as the average age of our farmers now hits the mid-50s, and *someone* has to grow our food. And such a 'disconnect', to borrow a slickness from the very spin doctors I'm maligning, also means most of us have little or no understanding of what it is to live beyond the urban buffer, even less how to address the problems out there that still need managing. So we regularly find ourselves applying city-wrought remedies to remote area issues and wondering why they won't come to heel.

And what we can't tame we ignore, or worse still, deceive ourselves we are correcting.

*Although this abbreviated version tends to be the accepted meaning, Marx was actually saying religion gave poor people a *much-needed* illusion of happiness, and was not necessarily making the negative observation it is usually perceived as. Seen in this light the analogy with consumerism resonates even more deeply.

**Bastardisation of "There is a tide in the affairs of men, Which, taken at the flood, leads on to fortune;" from the play Julius Caesar by William Shakespeare, spoken by Brutus when he is arguing their army must act now or risk defeat.

On most humanitarian levels Aboriginal Australia is worse off now than it was fifty years ago, and as each new government faces the challenge with absolute certainty its way is the only way, the situation grows more dire. But whichever way you look at it we're not winning, and it seems the best of State and Federal intentions from both sides of politics have done more harm than good. Perhaps it's time we conceded the current models simply aren't working and started getting those kids educated "*by any means necessary*", to quote the black American civil rights activist, Malcolm X. I'm not advocating another 'stolen generation', but let's open these protected enclaves up to the levelling influences of the wider Australian community, get serious about phasing out 'sit-down' money and stop tippy-toeing around the mess like kids at a broken window. And I include *all* Australians in this, for there is no more gain in victimhood than there is in racism, guilt, or welfare dependence.

"The Lucky Country" Donald Horne* was so critical of in his book of the same name back in 1964 prospers still, amidst the same blissful ignorance. We still rely heavily on our natural resources to see us right and most of us have no clue who owns what or where it goes, or care. So long as we maintain the standard of living, "She'll be right, mate." But common sense tells us this is no way to build national wealth. Instead of squandering our windfalls on tax benefits and stimulus packages that leave us with a boom-balanced economy

---

*The great irony with Horne's title, of course, is that the intended irony is usually overlooked in favour of the endearing connotation. The original sentence it came from ran, "Australia is a lucky country, run by second-rate people who share its luck." Before he died Horne complained, "I have had to sit through the most appalling rubbish as successive generations misapplied this phrase."

and nowhere to turn when the bust is on, why not invest a bit in infrastructure out there? I'm not deluding myself that the interior can be opened up with a few new roads and a hot dog stand, but surely we're smart enough to develop a *public* transport network on the back of private enterprise, aren't we? As a case in point we've recently seen port facilities and rail lines duplicated in the iron ore provinces of Western Australia because companies wouldn't share facilities. This is not merely an insane waste of resources but a good indication of the upside of boom time mining and what can be achieved when needs must. Take a firmer hand in these decisions and get a rail link built from Perth to Broome, for example, or another deep water port. Or let's get radical and think long-term like we used to and pipe the Ord water south. With ambition and foresight this could all be subsidised by the mining industry. No, not easy stuff, but certainly not impossible. Just ask Twiggy*.

And I'm dismayed to see we're losing the battle with our feral infestations. It looks to me like feral cats are here to stay and many of our native birds and animals will have to go. Forever. I also thought it was telling the Murchison pastoralist with the dog problem nominated kangaroos as his biggest threat, and I wonder if we aren't missing some obvious, albeit left-field solutions. Maybe we should be farming kangaroos on marginal land instead of the more environmentally demanding livestock? For that matter why not harvest dogs for meat? And put a real dollar value on cats and camels and donkeys and pigs and friends while we're at it. The feral goat industry has shown it can be done, and surely there

---

*Andrew Forrest, CEO of Fortescue Metals Group, the company that built its own rail link almost 300 kilometres to its own purpose-built deepwater port at Port Hedland because BHP Billiton and RIO Tinto refused to share.

are qualified markets to our north. Okay, so cane toads might be a bit of a trick, but I'm thinking the French colonies. *Cuisses de grenouilles la grande*, anyone? Irreverence aside, I can't think of one introduced pest in this country that we've managed to control effectively, and if what we're doing isn't working, do we just carry on with more of the same?

Yet please forgive me, I've snuck onto my soapbox and got carried away. Yes, like all countries, we have our problems. But what I set out to say was the country many of us think is out there is not more than a fraction of the one that awaits. Certainly it's still the land of almost incomprehensible extremes, of beauty so sublime at times it's hard to accept its capacity for proportionate devastation. And of course we have the luxury of space and a many-splendoured land with flora and fauna so unique they define us to the world as clearly as our passports. But for me it's about the people; all the misfits and marvels, fighters and fools, lovers and loons that defy mainstream and people the back pockets of our country. They are what give the bush heart and keep it alive. And for me, they are what make the Australian outback an infinitely fascinating journey beyond the homogeneity of urbanisation.

And did I find the H chord? Not this time. I may just have to go around again.

PREFERRED SUPPLIERS

Claude excelled himself on this trip. Big ticket items included: a fifth alternator (though I believe we've cured that problem now by installing a Nippon Denso with a double-varnished stator); a new set of house batteries (again victims of the rough treatment I dish out, hopefully cured with more secure fixings and heavier foam seating); one torsion bar (faulty or fatigued it's impossible to say, but blame it on the corrugations either way); one set of rear parabolic springs (put that down to Arnhem Land, upgraded to heavier leaf springs); a third set of front shocks (upgraded now to customised heavy duty Konis); one turbo charger (the old compressor fan chewed out by liquid gas hitting the blades as solid ice particles, corrected by replacing turbo and relocating gas assist intake); and one shot automatic transmission (probably due to overworking in high range and certainly contributing to the lack of power under load, corrected with an overhaul of transmission, torque converter and transfer case, plus the mobilisation of low range). Add to this lot sundry smaller problems such as another set of body mounts (Arnhem Land), a blown diff. lock actuator (which meant I drove right around the country totally oblivious I had no 4WD), the usual brakes and tyre maintenance issues, and various auto electrical puzzles that I'm disappointed to say were beyond many of our finest (I suspect because they're all so used to off-the-shelf servicing they've forgotten how to think, if not charge). However there were a few operators I came across prepared to offer that little bit extra to get the job done properly, or at very least provide a correct diagnosis and point me in the right direction, and I'm indebted to the following in:

Alice Springs - Ray Tebeck Auto Electrics;

Brisbane - Mike Vine Turbos, R&J Batteries;

Cairns - Cairns Spring Works & Engineering, Cape York Automotive, Knights Brakes, Casey's Battery Centre, FNQ Auto Electrics, and especially **Greg Struber** of **All Marine Electrics** (without whose experience and patience I'd be well and truly stuffed);

Darwin - Darwin Auto Electrics, All About Automotive, L&S Springs;

Laverton - Complete Services;

Mt Isa - K&B Diesel; and

Sydney - Jonesy's Wheel Alignment, APS Automatics, Sam Cali Mechanical Repairs.

Honourable mentions also to my mate Lex Bell in Clontarf, who always seems to "have something in the yard that might do the trick", in Perth the Smith family for the backyard service and my provider of discounted Khumo tyres whose business name I've forgotten, Peter Ondale in Holloways Beach for the great welding job on the busted torsion bar, Dwayne at Zebra Wreckers in Rockhampton for helping me look for the torsion bar that couldn't be found, Bob from Alternate Gas in Sydney for finding the fridge door that couldn't be found, Tom at Old Mac Toyota in Springwood for finding in Japan what couldn't be found in Australia, Kevin Anderson MP in Tamworth for access to his many, generous contacts, and all the bush mechanics and roadside assistants who offered help and humour in all the far flung, woe-begotten snake pits I've been stuck in around this country.

ABOUT THE AUTHOR

By his own admission Monte Dwyer is now unfit for polite society. He's been living the vagrant life so long he can barely remember *how* to behave, much less *care*. But he still believes in keeping things real and rails against mediocrity and the mainstream malaise. His media career has taken many turns and he was once a household name in Australia thanks to the stupefying powers of television, though these days he's happier running his own show as a wandering storyteller with an open brief. He believes in sunshine and the uncompromising freedom of the Australian bush, and when he grows up he wants to be satisfied he's done his best.